ESSAYS AND STUDIES
1981

ESSAYS AND STUDIES
1981

BEING VOLUME THIRTY-FOUR OF THE NEW SERIES
OF ESSAYS AND STUDIES COLLECTED FOR
THE ENGLISH ASSOCIATION

BY ANNE BARTON

HUMANITIES PRESS
ATLANTIC HIGHLANDS, N.J.

© The English Association 1981

Typeset by Inforum Ltd, Portsmouth,
printed and bound in Great Britain by
Fakenham Press Limited, Fakenham, Norfolk

ISBN 0-391-02292-X

Contents

I

Wyatt's Selfish Style

JOHN KERRIGAN

CHANGE and chance, Plato's busy dice, mutability, fortune, hap: these hold Wyatt's world in sway.[1] If his vision of sublunary uncertainty is not original (and something like it can be found in the work of many fourteenth and fifteenth century authors), his concerned focus on the individual inhabiting instability certainly is—at least in English literature. Chaucer, Lydgate and those early Tudor poets who followed Lydgate in the *De casibus* tradition were fascinated by Fortune because of her power over the destiny of all mankind. Wyatt was interested in her only in so far as she threatened the integrity of the particular self.

Indeed, one symptom of Wyatt's originality is the prominence which his poetry affords to 'hap' and 'unhap' at the expense of the blindfold wheel-spinning goddess.[2] Wyatt does use 'fortune'—often enough as a personification. But its derivatives—'fortunate' and 'unfortunate'—he avoids, evi-

[1] See, e.g., poems VI, XVIII, XXI, XXII, XXVII, XXIX, XXX, XXXIII, XXXV, XLII, XLVI, XLIX, LVIII, LXV, LXXIV, LXXVIII, LXXX, LXXXV, LXXXVI, LXXXVII, LXXXVIII, XC, XCII, XCVII, CII, CVII, CVIII, CX, CXIV, CXIX, CXX, CXXIII, CXXVI, CXXIX, CXXXII, CLXV, CLXVIII, CL in the first section ('*Poems in the Hand of Sir Thomas Wyatt, Poems with Revisions in His Hand, and Poems Attributed to Him in the Sixteenth Century*') of R.A. Rebholz's 'Penguin English Poets' ed. (Harmondsworth, 1978). I use Rebholz's ed. (invariably, to avoid authorship controversy as far as possible, its first section) throughout. Wyatt's sources are quoted from the texts printed in the commentary of Kenneth Muir and Patricia Thomson's *Collected Poems of Sir Thomas Wyatt* (Liverpool, 1969). I am grateful to The British Library for permission to publish manuscript material.

[2] See Eva Catherine Hangen, *A Concordance to the Complete Poetical Works of Sir Thomas Wyatt* (Chicago, 1941). The concordance is keyed to A.K. Foxwell's now superseded ed., but it will support a general point like this.

dently because, describing only the external circumstances of the self, they say nothing that cannot be said more decisively by their lexical parent. 'Hap' and 'unhap' on the other hand he uses as freely in their adjectival as in their substantival forms. And it is precisely their capacity to produce such derivatives that makes 'hap' and 'unhap' appeal to the poet. Their extension into 'happy and 'unhappy'—or into 'happiness' and its opposite—is an extension of circumstance into the self, an intrusion of instability. Nothing could be more economically typical of Wyatt than is the first stanza of LXXXVII, with its movement from 'Such hap as I am happed in' to the 'new kind of unhappiness' which is its consequence. The shift from 'If that my hap will hap so well' to 'thus unhappy must I serve' in the last stanza of CXXVI is of the same kind.

Perhaps the most striking example of this movement can be found in the sonnet 'The pillar perished'. Wyatt revises the very first line of his source, *'Rotta è l'alta colonna e 'l verde lauro'*. But it is quite understandable that he should quash Petrarch's shady laurel and call his column a 'pillar'.[3] The anonymous Tudor translator whose work survives in British Library Add. MS 36529—having, like Wyatt, no cause to lament the double loss of Laura and Giovanni Colonna—did the same. Lines 5–6, however (rendered conscientiously, if inadequately, as 'Deathe hathe be refte the worlds cheef glory heere/Who made the mind wt lief the more content', by the anonymous translator), Wyatt revised altogether more radically:

> The pillar perished is whereto I leant,
> The strongest stay of mine unquiet mind;
> The like of it no man again can find—
> From east to west still seeking though he went—
> To mine unhap, for hap away hath rent
> Of all my joy the very bark and rind,
> And I, alas, by chance am thus assigned
> Dearly to mourn till death do it relent.

---

[3] *OED* does not record 'column' before 1481, when Caxton was careful to gloss it, 'pyler'.

With the introduction of happed unhap Wyatt departs from his source irreversibly. In Petrarch, death bows the speaker with sorrow by depriving him of two people he has loved. In Wyatt, it is hap which produces (continuously outer and inner) unhap—though exactly what hap has taken from the 'I' is left unclear—and death, having been displaced, becomes the longed-for end of the poem's self's unquiet.

Fear of unhap and the search for inner calm: Wyatt's pre-occupations are closer to those of late classicism than to anything in the English middle ages, and it comes as no surprise to find him telling his son 'I wold Senek were your studye and Epictetus, bicaus it is litel to be euir in your bosome'[4] or giving Queen Katharine a translation (via Budé) of Plutarch's *De tranquillitate et securitate animi*.[5] In the poetry itself, his philosophical debts are betrayed by a series of verbal echoes. 'Mine unquiet mind' in the sonnet just quoted derives, like 'Quieter of mind' in LXXXI, from Wyatt's rendering of Plutarch's title: 'Of the Quyete of Mynde'. Again, the stanzaic poem 'Who list his wealth and ease retain', which would have had a refrain like '*Timor mortis conturbat me*' in the previous century,[6] adopts instead a tag from Seneca's *Phaedra*: '*circa Regna tonat*'. And the powerful lines beginning 'Stand whoso list upon the slipper top/Of court estates' are lifted bodily from the second chorus of *Thyestes*.

That Wyatt's affinities are specifically late-classical is worth emphasis: he has been misleadingly called 'Augustan' and, more particularly, 'Horatian'.[7] The wit ('Who expos'd to others Ey's,/Into his own Heart ne'r pry's,/Death to him 's a

---

[4] From a letter printed in Kenneth Muir, *Life and Letters of Sir Thomas Wyatt* (Liverpool, 1963), quoting p. 43. The small Epictetus which Wyatt has in mind is presumably Politian's Latin tr. of the *Encheiridion*.

[5] Rpt. as Appendix B of Muir and Thomson's ed.

[6] From the Office for the Dead. See, e.g., Lydgate's 'So as I lay this othir nyght', Dunbar's 'Lament for the Makars' and John Awdelaye's 'Dred of death'.

[7] Thomas Warton seems to have established this critical tradition. See his eloquent pages on Wyatt in *The History of English Poetry*, Vol. III (London, 1781).

Strange surprise') and urbanity ('Settled in some secret Nest /In Calm Leisure let me rest') which Marvell brings to his translation of the Thyestean chorus might be called 'Augustan'.[8] Wyatt's fearful heightening (death gripping man 'right hard by the crop' to leave him not surprised but 'dazed, with dreadful face') and his stark economy ('use me quiet')—these hardly could be. Nor does 'Horatian' seem right, even for the Satires with their echoes of the classical poet.[9] Although the first of them, 'Mine own John Poyntz', does initiate the tradition of English retirement poetry, the retreat to 'Kent and Christendom' recommended at the end of the piece is far from being Wyatt's final solution to the problem of unhap—whatever position 'Prouenza' occupies in the work of Alamanni.[10] In the second, Wyatt staunchly resists Horace's preference for the life of the country as opposed to that of the town mouse, judging both unhappy. He concludes that since 'Each kind of life hath with him his disease' (including, as it were, life on the Sabine farm) it is better to look within—to the resources of self—than without:

> Then seek no more out of thyself to find
>   The thing that thou hast sought so long before,
>   For thou shalt feel it sitting in thy mind.
>
> (97–9)

When he came to write his third and last Satire, Wyatt did not even entertain the idea that retirement might provide consolation for the virtuous public man. The same view, significantly enough, underlies his translation from *Thyestes*. Marvell makes Seneca's '*plebeius . . . senex*' a picturesque 'old honest

---

[8] 'Senec. Traged. ex Thyeste Chor. 2.', quoting from H.M. Margoliouth's ed. (Oxford, 1927). Marvell is translating '*Obscuro positus loco/ Leni perfruar otio*' and '*Illi mors gravis incubat/Qui notus nimis omnibus/Ignotus moritur sibi*'.

[9] On these debts see Rebholz, pp. 437, 445 and 449–50, and Ch. viii of Patricia Thomson, *Sir Thomas Wyatt and His Background* (London, 1964).

[10] Luigi Alamanni's *Satira X* (pub. 1532) provided most of the content as well as the *terza rima* form of Wyatt's poem.

Country man'; Wyatt extinguishes him in the vague 'common trace'. Marvell's poem is effectively an 'Horatian' celebration of rural retreat from 'the publick Stage'; Wyatt's, by contrast, advocates (notably in lines 8–10) a retreat within, to a Delphic knowledge of self.

The recoil into self which rings clear in a phrase like 'use me quiet' (hewn out of 'use my life in quietness' in Wyatt's draft)[11] can be found everywhere. In an extreme poem like 'Madam, withouten many words' (an offer of love so curtly self-assertive that it provoked a contemporary rebuke)[12] Wyatt's recoil is so strong that it carries text back into an ellipsis:

> If it be yea I shall be fain.
> If it be nay friends as before.
> Ye shall another man obtain
> And I mine own and yours no more.

('I mine own' what?)[13] More often, a smooth conveyance of sense is disrupted by the insistent foregrounding of a first person pronoun. These examples are from the Penitential Psalms: 'I, Lord, am strayed. I sick without recure' (97), 'I, for because I hid it still within' (237), ' "I shall," quod I, "against myself confess" ' (254), 'I sinner, I! What have I said, alas?' (514), 'I know that helpless I should drown' (577).

But there are two poems—one dealing with self-loss and the other with self-gain—which convey particularly well both the strength of Wyatt's centripetal instinct and its capacity to inform the most unlikely parts of his work. In the first, the rondeau 'Help me to seek for I lost it there', Wyatt presents the conventionally playful motif of the lady's possession of her lover's heart with an almost-physical anguish:

---

[11] The whole draft is printed by Rebholz (pp. 371–2).

[12] The poem 'Of few words, sir, you seem to be', written as an answer to Wyatt's in the Egerton and Blage MSS.

[13] 'Man', presumably, and so (with the silent 'obtain') without much reduction, 'self '.

Help me to seek for I lost it there;
And if that ye have found it, ye that be here,
And seek to convey it secretly,
Handle it soft and treat it tenderly
Or else it will plain and then appair.

A poet like Charles D'Orleans (I am thinking of his masterly rondeau, 'Go forth myn hert wyth my lady') delights in the gift; Wyatt feels it an intolerable dissolution of self. Compare the epigram 'In doubtful breast', in which Wyatt treats Mary—the mother who devoured her child in the siege of Jerusalem—with complete sympathy. It's not, apparently, that he blames the Jews for taking her food, or that he accepts that the mother had a right to end the sufferings of her son (the feelings which lurk beneath the sensationalist surface of Nashe's account),[14] but that he is moved by Mary's recovery of a portion of self. The interesting lines are the last four:

'Yield me those limbs that I made unto thee
And enter there where thou wert generate.
For of one body against all nature
To another must I make sepulture.'

Nothing could be further from the coldly clever '*si come da me fur fatte sian disfatte*' of the source strambotto than 'enter there where thou wert generate', with its calm and engorging 'er' assonances (five of them) and ambiguous 'enter' ('inter' being drawn out by the epigrammatical paradox generated by 'generate' and by the poem's last word)[15]—both working to make it seem perfectly natural (for all the mother's protestation to the contrary) that what was once 'generate' should 'enter' and

[14] In *Christs Teares Over Iervsalem*. See *The Works of Thomas Nashe*, ed. R.B. McKerrow (rpt. Oxford, 1958), Vol. II, pp. 71–7.
[15] On the phonetic and orthographic basis of this ambiguity see E.J. Dobson, *English Pronunciation 1500-1700*, 2nd ed. (Oxford, 1968), Vol. I, p. 412, and *OED* 'inter'.

'inter' itself where it began to be, that the self should reclaim itself.

*

How does Wyatt's sympathy for (let us call it) selfishness affect the way he writes? I would compare the poetry with the Holbein sketch. The impassive (self-possessed) face of the artist's Wyatt is guarded by a pair of intelligent eyes which, refusing to engage with those which view them, look warily beyond at the untrustworthy world. (Contrast Holbein's Surrey.) The selves of the poetry (those versions of Wyatt precipitated in art) similarly exclude enquiring Is while rebuking the world (part 'Is'', part Is') for fickleness.[16] A Wyatt poem is typically plain (advertising the sincerity of its self in a world that is otherwise) and extraordinarily opaque (reserving that self to itself). The poet characterized his manner well when, looking for an image to express the beauty of his ideal mistress' face, he (and so the 'I' of LXVII) found it reflexively in expression: 'With sober cheer so would I that it should/Speak, without words, such words that none can tell.'

Certainly, 'The pillar perished' is not the only poem in which Wyatt writes fervently about a situation which is left more or less without words. 'They flee from me', for example, speaks most eloquently not through what it says but through what it leaves silent. Consider the obliquity with which we are introduced to the predicament of its 'I': as we read into the second stanza we realize that the plural animal flight which the first had offered as the self's loss is only an image of a loss which remains essentially unspoken. Emphasizing the ignorance in which he leaves us (something as much increased as reduced by the painfully direct, ' "Dear heart, how like you this?" '), Wyatt ends the poem with an enquiry ('I would fain know what she hath deserved') which disturbs and haunts precisely because we are in no position to answer it—however much we discover about jesses, the feeding habits of the deer

---

[16] This is not the place to defend the unfashionably pre-Derridean assumptions which underlie the latter part of this essay.

and Anne Boleyn.

The temptation to put biography into the silences of Wyatt's poetry is very strong (especially, I suspect, for those who are moved by it); but since the poetry speaks by not saying then it must be sternly resisted. Take, for example, the famous lines:

> The bell tower showed me such sight
> That in my head sticks day and night.
> There did I learn out of a grate,
> For all favour, glory, or might,
> That yet *circa Regna tonat*.

All recent Wyatt editors assert or imply that the 'sight' which wrought such havoc on the 'I' of CXXIII was the execution of Anne Boleyn.[17] And so we start to muse: 'I can see her as distinctly as if I were there. Ah, how beautiful she looks! and how she moves all hearts to pity! Suffolk, Richmond, Cromwell, and the Lord Mayor are there to meet her . . . She rises. The fatal moment is at hand. Even now she retains her courage—she approaches the block, and places her head upon it. The axe is raised——'. Then we stop short, recalling that the editors have no solid grounds for their identification and that one is admitting these fancies (they are Harrison Ainsworth's)[18] in defiance of the poem's secretive self-centredness—or, rather, in an unjustified reaction against the secretively self-centred poem's defiance of us.

The other two poems which seem to have grown out of the traumatic experiences of 1536 and 1541 are no more responsive to biographical interpretation. The better of them, the epigram 'Sighs are my food', is almost bare of the contingent details of prison life which such criticism needs if it is to find purchase; tight form and syntax are the massy walls which the

---

[17] Muir and Thomson are more positive than Joost Daalder (Oxford, 1975) and Rebholz, even though they concede that their only witness (the *Crónica del Rey Enrico*) is untrustworthy.
[18] *Windsor Castle* (1843), Bk. VI, Ch. viii.

'I' of this poem is under and between. And in the double sonnet 'The flaming sighs that boil within my breast' the centring is so decisive—not prison but the self is here the place of drama: 'he that list to see and to discern/How care ~~can~~ force within a wearied mind,/Come he to me: I am that place assigned'—that it is very easy to follow Tottel in assuming that the 'I' is not in prison but, like so many of his unhappy fellows, in love.[19] To find a poet speaking out, rather than in, about early sixteenth-century prison life, a poet with some sense of the black absurdity of confinement, we have to abandon Wyatt and turn to Marot—whose *L'Enfer*, with its assimilation of Lucianic burlesque to medieval personification allegory, also reminds us how much Wyatt's plainness depends on an avoidance both of classical allusion and the vigorous personification mode employed to such effect by Skelton and the morality dramatists.[20]

On occasion, Wyatt's 'I' frankly retreats behind a riddle. There is that routine bawdy conundrum, 'A lady gave me a gift she had not', and the poem so beloved of biographers, 'What word is that that changeth not/Though it be turned and made in twain?' ('Anna'); and there is the acrostic on Lady Stanhope (LXVI). But it could be argued that Wyatt's reticence makes all his poems, to some degree, riddles. 'They flee from me' is as much a puzzle as a poem (hence the last, questioning line); so is 'Perdie, I said it not'; and in CIII the bewilderment of the speaker within the poem is disturbingly extended to the reader by the double-edged recurring query, 'What means this?' Indeed, the riddling assumption is so strong in Wyatt that the poet is able, from time to time, to baffle the reader by simplicity. In 'Me list no more to sing', for example, the message is straightforwardly *'Carpe diem'*; but a suggestion of cunning concealment in the last stanza (with that characteristic recoil into the selfish 'I')—

[19] In *Tottel's Miscellany* (1557–87), the title is 'The lover describeth his restless state'.

[20] The exceptions—'Apollo' and the 'spindle of my fate' in LXXVI, 'Favel' in CXLIX and a few others—only prove the rule.

> If this be under mist
> And not well plainly wist,
> Understand me who list
> For I reck not a bean;
> I wot what I do mean.

—is enough to force the reader fruitlessly back over the text to discover just 'What means this?'

'Me list no more to sing', in common with many of Wyatt's poems, gives the impression that it is unfolding, not given. The 'I' sings of its songs in general, promises that the song it is now singing is different and then suggests that, after all, it may not be so unlike the songs formerly mistook. More interested in their own expression than in their audience, Wyatt's selfish selves seem to be constantly addressed to their singing and saying: 'I have cause good to sing this song' (LIX), 'Therefore this song thy fault to thee it sings' (XXXVII), 'And yet, with more delight to moan my woeful case,/I must complain those hands, those arms that firmly do embrace/Me from myself ' (LXXVI).[21] In extreme cases, such as CXXVIII or CIX, the selves underline their unwillingness to utter (outer) themselves by introducing a lute as an alternative audience (the song's agent becoming its ear). On the one hand, Wyatt's use of this kind of performative reflexivity authenticates his selves (one thinks of the troubadour 'I').[22] On the other, because the poems unfold according to their own rules (not, inevitably, to those of an 'I's' spontaneous utterance), they are simultaneously detached from the (by convention) creative selves (which they create). The verse is recessional: the Wyatt 'I' interposes between itself

[21] 'Moan' and 'complain' were added (like the infolding 'Me from myself') to Petrarch, who only weeps.

[22] I mean that in many troubadour lyrics the poetry seems 'fresh' and 'personal' because the author has included an 'I' ostensibly in the act of creation: William IX's *'Farai un vers de dreyt nïen . . . Fag ai lo vers, no say de cuy'* ('I'll make a poem from downright nothingness . . . I've made this poem, I don't know of what') and Marcabrun's *'Cortesamen vuoill comenssar/ Un vers, si es qui l'escout'ar,/E puios tant m'en sui entremes,/Veirai si.l poirai affinar'* ('I want to start a poem in the courtly style if there's anyone to hear. And since I'm in so far, I'll see if I can make it fine') are typical.

and the reader poetry which—being so much about its own unfolding—yields remarkably little about that self.

The exclusion of the enquiring I effected by this interposition is particularly apparent in 'My lute awake!' The song is (by convention) personal and sincere: it is 'My song'. But it is also, as 'this song', distinctly independent of the 'I'. And so concerned is it with itself—with its own process (stanzas 1, 8 and the first lines of 2) and its agent (the lute)—that the circumstances in which the 'I' finds itself, its reasons for feeling justified in calling for 'Vengeance', these are left almost without words. Why is this poem so much more successful than the lyrics which surround it? Because, I would argue, Wyatt's abiding stylistic selfishness here harmonizes perfectly with a subject (both senses): the despairing introspection of the (which is the) rejected lover. It also succeeds because although the poem excludes enquiring Is from its 'I' it nevertheless engages them in a drama of response: our eagerness, as hearers of the song and as bearers in our hearts of its gradually extending impress (I have in mind lines 6–8), both to listen to and to discover the nature of the emotions which prompt the song, contrasts sharply with the unhearing and stony-hearted indifference of the mistress.

It is no accident that Wyatt made such use of that previously rare (at least in English) form, the rondeau: he was strongly attracted to circularity—poems with tails in their mouths, verse like the posy of a ring—because it gave expression (in a way which statement, by nature revealing, clearly could not) to poems' selves' selfishness. Sometimes he creates an effect of complex struggle between threat and defence by employing and drawing attention to the employment of this device. In 'Who list his wealth and ease retain', for example,[23] the return of 'innocency' (stanza 5) to the 'Innocentia' which heads the epigraph (image of the self's essential integrity) is only the largest circle described (both senses) by a poem which with its circling refrain about circling ('circa Regna tonat'), begins with a motto which rings the 'I' ('Viat') with its virtues ('Innocentia/

---

[23] Other examples are I and LXXXVII.

Veritas . . . Fides') and then laments its further encirclement by its foes: *'Circumdederunt me inimici mei'*. More often Wyatt's aim is exclusion: his poetry, closing into itself (and completing the expression of its content in form), insists on privacy. Here again 'My lute awake!' succeeds because it correlates a stylistic habit with a subject: the song's 'I's' singing returns to its beginning at its end (compare the first and last stanzas) because as far as its attempt to stir the conscience of the absent mistress is concerned it might as well not have been. 'As to be heard where ear is none,/As lead to grave in marble stone,/My song may pierce her heart as soon': the song must 'lead' (as it sings of graving lead) to the 'grave' of its circularity.[24]

What can criticism do with such poetry? Not much, except point to the pathos of its closure, and to the poignancy with which it completes in form its simple message of forsakenness. Even if it is based on the soundest precepts of the best literary theorists, a more contextual interpretation—attending to the poetry's biographical, historical or literary historical envelope—will be poorly rewarded:

> When Pantagruel had read the superscription, he was much amazed and therefore demanded of the said messenger the name of her that had sent it: then opened he the letter, and found nothing written in it, nor otherwayes inclosed, but only a gold ring, with a square table-diamond. Wondering at this, he called Panurge to him, and shewed him the case; whereupon Panurge told him, that the leafe of paper was written upon, but with such cunning and artifice, that no man could see the writing at the first sight, therefore to find it out he set it by the fire, to see if it was made with Sal Ammoniack soaked in water; then put he it into the water, to see if the letter was written with the juice of Tithymalle: after that he held it up against the candle, to see if it was written with the juice of white onions.
>
> Then he rubbed one part of it with oile of nuts, to see if it were not written with the lee of a fig-tree: and another part of it with the milk of a woman giving suck to her eldest daughter, to see if it was written with the blood of red toads, or green earth-frogs:

---

[24] On the phonetic basis of this (glimmer of a) pun, see E.J. Dobson, *op. cit.*, Vol. II, pp. 503 and 775.

Afterwards he rubbed one corner with the ashes of a Swallowes nest, to see if it were not written with the dew that is found within the herb Alcakengie, called the winter-cherry. He rubbed after that one end with eare-wax, to see if it were not written with the gall of a Raven: then did he dip it into vineger, to try if it was not written with the juice of the garden Spurge: After that he greased it with the fat of a bat or flitter-mouse, to see if it was not written with the sperm of a whale, which some call ambergris: then put it very fairly into a basin full of fresh water, and forthwith took it out, to see whether it were written with stone-allum. . .

Then he said to Pantagruel, Master, by the vertue of G— I cannot tell what to do nor say in it; for . . . I have made use of a good part of that which Master Francisco di Nianto, the Tuscan sets down . . . that which Zoroastes published, *Peri grammaton acriton*; and Calphurnius Bassus, *de literis illegibilibus*: but I can see nothing, nor do I beleeve that there is any thing else in it then the Ring: let us, therefore, look upon it. Which when they had done, they found this in Hebrew written ithin, *Lamach sabathani* . . . words signifying, Wherefore hast thou forsaken me? upon that Panurge suddenly replied, I know the mystery, do you see this diamond? it is a false one; this, then is the exposition of that which the Lady meanes, *Diamant faux*, that is, false lover, why hast thou forsaken me?[25]

*

Why did Wyatt write? Why, if he was so concerned to make even his poetic selves secretive, did he not leave his lute in its case? The obvious renaissance reply, 'for fame', might help with that 'other Adonis', Skelton (his gown embroidered 'Calliope'),[26] and it might go some way towards explaining the phenomenon of Marot or the poetry of the Pléiade. It will not do for Wyatt. Compare this (the final stanza of Ronsard's

[25] From Ch. xxiv of Rabelais' *Pantagruel* (1532), quoting from the rpt. of Urquhart's tr. in 'The Tudor Translations' (London, 1900).

[26] The epigraph to 'The Garland of Laurel' includes the following: '*Hinc nostrum celebre et nomen referetur ad astra,/Undique Skeltonis memorabitur alter Adonis.*' On Skelton's gown, see H.L.R. Edwards' biography (London, 1949), p. 37, and Maurice Pollet's, tr. John Warrington (London, 1971), p. 66, as well as the poem, 'Calliope'.

'A Sa Lire'), with the quietly involuted last lines of 'My lute awake!':[27]

> Par toi je plai, & par toi je suis leu,
> C'est toi qui fais que Ronsard soit éleu
> Harpeur François, & quant on le rencontre
> Qu'avec le doi par la rue on le montre:
> Si je plai donc, si je sçai contanter,
> Si mon renom la France veut chanter,
> Si de mon front les étoilles je passe,
> Certes mon Luc cela vient de ta grace.

Even if Wyatt invited us to identify him with the 'I' of his lyric (which, of course, he does not), it could hardly be claimed that 'Wyatt' was offered to the gaze of eternity in the same spirit as Ronsard's 'Ronsard'. Certainly, there is no suggestion that the 'Viat' of 'Who list his wealth and ease retain' is bidding for fame.[28] Indeed, there is some evidence that Wyatt viewed literary renown with positive distaste. He not only avoids mentioning present and future fame in his own verse, but avoids translating poems—of which there are a number in the Canzoniere—which make such fame an important theme. Coming upon the merely glancing reference to Petrarch's fame in 'Quell'antiquo mio dolce empio signore' ('Mine old dear en'my'), Wyatt suppressed it rather than have it attributed to his 'I'.[29] But this is what we would expect. Because Wyatt's self-assertiveness combined with a profound distrust of the world beyond the self, an apparent paradox was produced: his selves centre to the point of anonymity. It is hardly surprising that the canon is so ill-defined.

[27] The date of composition of Wyatt's lyric is uncertain; it was recorded in the Egerton MS in the mid-1530s. Ronsard composed his poem in 1549 and it was published in the following year. I quote from André Barbier's ed. of Ronsard (Oxford, 1946).

[28] This is the only poem in which Wyatt's name certainly appears. It has been suggested that the (unascribed) CLXXX conceals 'Wyatt' in the form of an anagram in the first letters of each stanza (T–A–W–I–T).

[29] Cf. Rime 360, ll. 88–9, LXXIII, ll. 81–2. Wyatt's handling of Petrach's ll. 110–20 is also relevant.

Why, then, did Wyatt write? Because, I believe, he regarded *poesis* as inherently ethical. Playful, alluring, shifty and deceitful, language was for him the self's most valuable inheritance from the unstable world and also its most fearful. Its instability—its windy freedom—obsessed him. He returned to the theme again and again, not only in the poetry ('words mutable', VI; 'The windy words . . . Of sudden change maketh me aghast', LXXXV; 'my sparkling voice', XIII; 'my words . . . they sparkle in the wind', XCVII), but also in writing which stands at the edge of his creative work (on crucial pages of 'To the Iudges after the Indictement', for example).[30] But—and this is where *poesis* comes in—the mutable word is not quite beyond control: it can be fixed by form. Poetry wrests stability out of flux. It builds a pillar for the unquiet mind in the middle of hap's domain. That, in the last analysis, is the reason why Wyatt wrote. It is also the reason why even his most despairing selves (the 'I' of 'My lute awake!', for example) sing their songs. If the self's words cannot pierce the heart of an obdurate mistress, they can unfold a consoling achievement.

Wyatt's most chaste and lovely poem (so productive of biographical Panurgism)[31] seems to me crucially concerned with that quest for verbal stability which lies at the heart of Wyatt's imaginative life. For all its lack of explicitly performative reflexivity, it is very much about its achievement—and its limitations—as poetry:

> Whoso list to hunt, I know where is an hind,
> But as for me, helas, I may no more.
> The vain travail hath wearied me so sore,
> I am of them that farthest cometh behind.

---

[30] *Life and Letters*, pp. 187–209, esp. pp. 196–206.

[31] The identification of the hind with Anne Boleyn (see, e.g. E.K. Chambers, *Sir Thomas Wyatt and Some Collected Studies* [London, 1933], p. 132, and Sergio Baldi, *La Poesia di Sir Thomas Wyatt* [Florence, 1953], pp. 18–19, 22, 57) has no visible means of support. The implication that the poem dates from as early as 1526–7 (when Henry VIII claimed Anne) is particularly unattractive.

Yet may I by no means my wearied mind
Draw from the deer, but as she fleeth afore
Fainting I follow. I leave off therefore
Sithens in a net I seek to hold the wind.
Who list her hunt, I put him out of doubt,
As well as I may spend his time in vain.
And graven with diamonds in letters plain
There is written her fair neck round about:
'*Noli me tangere* for Caesar's I am,
And wild for to hold though I seem tame.'

As far as the verse of mortals may, this catches wind in a net
and holds the wild thing. But there is text in it which is stable
beyond the powers of the hunting 'I' and of the poet behind
that 'I'. The mysterious and yet 'plain' words on the hind's
neck are written in diamonds (emblem of constancy as well as
of price) and—this being Wyatt—they close into a circle
('written her fair neck round about'). They are also Divine. It is
most significant that Wyatt replaced the vernacular of Petrarch's '*Nessun mi tocchi*' with chiselled-out Vulgate Latin and
traced '*Libera farmi al mio Cesare parve*' back to its origin in
Matthew 22:21. Both revisions go a long way towards
explaining why Wyatt translated the Penitential Psalms.

In the word of God, Wyatt finally found absolute stability,[32]
an unperishable pillar (the description cuts free of the
sources)[33] for the (his, the 'I's') unquiet mind:

Thy holy word of eterne excellence,
Thy mercy's promise that is alway just,
Have been my stay, my pillar, and pretence.
(685–7)

How remarkable, and yet how predictable in view of the (to
use that barbarism again) performative reflexivity of the secu-
lar poetry, that Wyatt's 'I' should sing so—should sing of the

[32] I intend 'finally' in a logical rather than chronological sense, though a
late date of composition (1541 rather than 1536) seems to me very probably
correct.
[33] See Muir and Thomson's note to ll. 680–7.

stability that resides in God's word in a song which, being
Holy Writ, *is* God's 'word stable' (452). It is easy to see why
the poet was attracted to Aretino's narrative framework,
showing, as it does, 'David' and his harp (religious equivalents
of Wyatt's 'I' and his lute) creating the Psalms as the Psalms
proceed. It is easy to see, too, why Wyatt tightened the links
between 'David' and his song by adding to Aretino a string of
references to the word. The following is typical:

> My heart, my mind is withered up like hay
> Because I have forgot to take my bread,
> My bread of life, the word of truth, I say.
>
> (553–5)

Wyatt's gloss, 'the word of truth', is intensely Protestant. In
the light of this addition to Aretino at least, the poet was right
to protest to his judges, against the accusation that he had
passed state intelligence to Cardinal Pole, that 'I thynke I
shulde have more adoe with a great sorte in Inglande to purge
my selffe of suspecte of a Lutherane then of a Papyst'.[34] But the
gloss is also continuous, in terms of poetic method, with the
kind of attention paid to words in the love songs.

  And yet, there is a difference, and it is crucial. As the
swan-song (XCVIII), 'To wish and want and not obtain' or 'My
lute awake!' attend to their singing, they involve despairingly,
consoling the 'I' only by their achievement. The 'I' of the
Psalms, however (like the biblical David and Tudor Wyatt
who conspire in that 'I'), precisely by attending to the word of
God which is unfolding in his song, quests beyond the word
(beyond the quest of the 'I' in 'Whoso list to hunt') to the
ultimate source of that word, the Word:

> This word 'redeem' that in his mouth did sound
> Did put David, it seemeth unto me,
> As in a trance to stare upon the ground
> And with his thought the height of heeven to see,

---

[34] *Life and Letters*, pp. 195–6.

Where he beholds the Word that should confound
The sword of death, by humble ear to be
In mortal maid, in mortal habit made,
Eternal life in mortal veil to shade.

He seeth that Word, when full ripe time should come,
Do way that veil by fervent affection,
Torn off with death (for death should have her doom),
And leapeth lighter from such corruption
Than glint of light that in the air doth lome.
Man redeemed, death hath her destruction,
That mortal veil hath immortality,
David assurance of his iniquity.

(695–710)

The progress of the Penitential Psalms, far from being despairingly involuted, is transcendent. In this, the climactic narrative
link, Wyatt moves rapturously from the last words of the 'De
profundis' to the Word which inspires them, exalting Aretino's
'la parola di Dio dal Cielo' into God Himself.

This is not offered as a deconstruction of Wyatt's faith. I
want to explain why a troubled spirit—fearful of change and
chance, Plato's busy dice, mutability, fortune, hap—found
consolation beyond poetry in the Word that can 'Speak, without words, such words that none can tell': Love never forsaken, the fulfilment of self in an anonymous eternity, stability, quiet.

II

Sincerity and the Sonnet

INGA–STINA EWBANK

This above all—to thine own self be true,
And it must follow, as the night the day,
Thou canst not then be false to any man.

(Hamlet, I,iii,78–80)

I am that I am.

(Shakespeare, sonnet 121)

I am not I, pitie the tale of me.

(Astrophil and Stella, 45)[1]

I

WHAT, or who, is a sincere sonneteer? When Ernest de Selin-
court edited the *Amoretti* as part of Spenser's *Minor Poems* in
1910, he was moved to lament that 'modern criticism' had
made 'so damaging an onslaught upon the sincerity of the
Elizabethan sonneteers'.[2] The history of literary criticism has
moved on since then, to a point where no one would dare
think that the poetic sincerity of the sonneteers is to be meas-
ured by their autobiographical accuracy, nor their originality
by their independence of literary models. We know now to

---

[1] Here, as in the rest of the essay, I use the Peter Alexander text of
Shakespeare (*The Complete Works*, London and Glasgow, 1951) and William
A. Ringler, Jr.'s text of *The Poems of Sir Philip Sidney* (Oxford, 1962).

[2] 'Introduction', p. xxiv. The 'modern criticism' would be best represented by Sir Sidney Lee, whose edition of *Elizabethan Sonnets* had
appeared in 1904, and who spent much of his life 'in attempting to prove that
all Elizabethan sonneteers were slavish imitators of foreign models rather
than men in love' (Kenneth Muir, *Shakespeare's Sonnets*, London, 1979, p.
30).

separate Sir Philip Sidney from Astrophil's claim that, 'loving in truth', he looks in his heart and writes; and we know that not William Shakespeare but the poet's *persona* claims to be 'true in love' and 'but truly write'. Literary sincerity, we presumably agree, is not a matter of there being no gap between the writer's avowed and actual feeling, but of his ability to create in the reader the impression of genuine feeling. Who is to say that the poet in Vernon Scannell's sonnet 'Love Poet' is not sincere?

> Of all the poets of his generation
> He best explored love's ecstasy and pain
> And overheard the wordless conversation
> Of gaze to gaze and made its meaning plain.
> In shining lyrics, delicate and witty,
> He linked the syllables and forged a chain
> Of images of sensual greed and pity
> That glittered in each reader's heart and brain.
> His tolerance and reconciliation
> Of opposites most critics deemed divine;
> Imagine then the general consternation
> When he fell sick, grew pale, began to pine
> And failed to diagnose his own condition:
> On love he never wrote another line.[3]

And yet there is food for thought in this little poem about an inverse relationship between feeling and expression and, at the heart of it, a faulty self-knowledge.

This essay is simply a gathering of some thoughts on ways in which the problems of sincerity—of knowing yourself and your 'true' feelings, expressing them 'truly', and thereby creating 'true' art—are explored and exploited in some of the major Elizabethan sonnet sequences. Its narrow room forces me to concentrate on Sidney, but other sonneteers, and Shakespeare in particular, will help to illuminate the problems he faces—and superbly solves. The problems are, of course,

---

[3] In *Of Love and Music* (Mapletree Private Press, 1980). I am grateful to the author and the Press for allowing me to quote this poem.

partly inherent in literary history itself, which presented the
would-be sonneteer with the challenge of an apparent paradox: an opportunity to 'voice personality'[4] and a conventional-
ized form and language to do so in. When Wyatt 'translates'
Petrarch's lament for the death of his patron (*'Rotta è l'alta
colonna* . . .') into an expression of his own grief on the execution of Thomas Cromwell ('The pillar pearisht is . . .'), it is
natural for him to move his attention inwards, to end, not with
Petrarch's haunting contemplation of the condition of man
(*'O nostra vita* . . .'), but with a sharp realization of his own
psychological state:

> And I my self, my self always to hate,
> Till dreadfull death do ease my dolefull state.[5]

The genius of the English sonnet, as J.W. Lever and others
have shown, was for such inward thrusts, towards anatomies
of selves. One would have thought that self-analysis spelled
expansiveness, especially when one remembers the lengths to
which the dramatic heroes of the 1580s and 90s go to voice
their love or grief. But the true sonneteer clearly found, as
Wordsworth was to do, that 'the prison, unto which we
doom/Ourselves, no prison is'. If we set beside each other
Hieronimo's famous lament 'O eyes, no eyes, but fountains
fraught with tears' and Sidney's sonnet 100, 'O teares, no
teares, but raine from beautie's skies'—written within a few
years of each other, and in a superficially similar rhetorical
pattern—we see that Hieronimo uses nearly twice as many
lines as Astrophil to complete his figure, and even then he has
merely expressed his sense of outraged justice. Astrophil cov-
ers far more emotional ground, from the lilies and the roses of
his tearful mistress to 'the hell where my soule fries' and back
to the 'perfect Musike' of her 'sobd out words'; and the paral-
lels and contrasts of his figure are structured into a purposeful
progress towards a cathartic oxymoron:

[4] J.W. Lever, *The Elizabethan Love Sonnet* (London, 1956), p. 143.
[5] *Collected Poems of Sir Thomas Wyatt*, ed. Kenneth Muir and Patricia
Thomson (Liverpool, 1969), p. 238.

Such teares, sighs, plaints, no sorrow is, but joy:
Or if such heavenly signes must prove annoy,
All mirth farewell, let me in sorrow live.

A sonnet like this may well strike us more by the ingenuity of
its conceits and its construction than by the sincerity of its
self-analysis. It shows the allure of what F.T. Prince has called
the 'sustained inevitability' of the sonnet method of discourse,[6] and it shows the English ability to use this method: to
argue through conceits ('O teares, no teares, but raine from
beautie's skies,/Making those Lillies and those Roses grow'),
to condense emotions into wordplay ('While graceful pitty
beauty beautifies'), and to tighten conclusions into epigrams.
It also shows that the problem which the sonnet posed to
sincerity was not how to avoid the strait-jacket (for sheer
scope there was after all the sequence) but how to resist the
temptations of automatic writing. We see those temptations
unresisted all too often in the spate of sonnet collections which
followed upon the first publication of *Astrophil and Stella*
(1591). But even Sidney, writing in the early 1580s, felt he had
to assert his poetic identity and the uniqueness of his experience by crying out against conventional sonneteering, as did
Shakespeare after him.

Not everyone did. At one extreme Spenser seems to have
found, within the convention, his own voice for idealizing his
first cruel and then happily responsive lady, and for celebrating the near-sacramental nature of their ultimate relationship.
Of introspection as such there is little or nothing in the
Amoretti. At the other extreme, Fulke Greville equally unself-
consciously ignores the sonnet convention whenever he wants
to, breaking through the form itself in the process (only
forty-one of the so-called sonnets which make up his sequence, *Caelica*, are true sonnets) and searching his own 'dark-
ened mind' with a disillusioned directness which defies any
questioning of his sincerity:

[6] F.T. Prince, 'The Sonnet from Wyatt to Shakespeare', in *Elizabethan
Poetry, Stratford-upon-Avon Studies*, II (London, 1960), pp. 11–29.

Within which minde since you from thence ascended,
Truth clouds it selfe, Wit serues but to resemble,
Enuie is King, at others good offended,
Memorie doth worlds of wretchednesse assemble,
Passion to ruin passion is intended,
My reason is but power to dissemble;
   Then tell me *Love*, what glory you diuine
   Your selfe can finde within this soule of mine?

                          (*Caelica*, 10)[7]

Greville's *forte* is to leave us disturbed, as when the final
'Chorus Sacerdotum' of his tragedy *Mustapha*, beginning
from the 'wearisome Condition of Humanity', takes us in the
closing lines into the individual mind:

   Yet when each of us, in his owne heart lookes,
   He findes the God there, farre unlike his Bookes.

Inverting the customary sonnet themes, he writes in *Caelica* of
change, of inconstancy, of love as creating chaos in the mind
and distorting reality ('Love is no true made *Looking-
glasse*/Which perfect yeelds the shape we bring,/It ugly showes
us all that was/And flatters euery future thing.' *Caelica*, 61).
When he looks in his heart, his vision is not like Sidney's, more
like Yeats's 'foul rag-and-bone shop'.[8] Yet it would be wrong
to conclude from his example that the only sincere sonnet is
the anti-sonnet. It would be wrong, too, to take out of context
a claim like Drayton's, in the prefatory sonnet to the 1619
edition of *Idea*, that 'My Verse is the true Image of my Mind',
and that (with a favourite Sidney adjective) 'No farre-fetch'd
Sigh shall ever wound my Brest'.[9] As the revisions, omissions
and additions in the various versions of *Idea* show us, his mind

---

[7] *Poems and Dramas of Fulke Greville, First Lord Brooke*, ed. Geoffrey
Bullough, 2 vols. (Edinburgh and London, 1939), I, p. 78.
[8] 'The Circus Animals' Desertion', in *The Collected Poems of W.B. Yeats*
(2nd ed., London, 1950), p. 392.
[9] *The Works of Michael Drayton*, ed. J. William Hebel, 5 vols (Oxford,
1931–41), II (1932), 310. This sonnet was first printed (as no. 2) in the 1599 ed.
of *Idea*; it became no. 1, 'To the Reader', in the 1605 ed.

was a sponge, soaking up traditions as well as innovations; and he might more truly have said that his verse is the true image of his predecessors'. In effect he unwittingly says so when, in his closing couplet, he moves away from the mind to the tradition with which he identifies himself: 'My Muse is rightly of the *English* straine'.

We know that, among Continental writers, criticism of Petrarchan conventions had in itself become a convention;[10] and we do not take literally the sonneteers' claim to sincerity and originality. Yet, a fear of committing the intentional fallacy should not obscure the fact that, from within the fiction of Sidney's and Shakespeare's sequences, these claims are made so insistently and with such an obsessive stress on the true voice of feeling as in Shakespeare's sonnet 82:

> Thou truly fair wert truly sympathiz'd
> In true plain words by thy true-telling friend.

Shakespeare is attacking here the insincerity of other poets' 'gross painting' and foreswearing 'What strained touches rhetoric can lend', much as Sidney had scorned the 'daintie wits' who 'crie on the Sisters nine,/That bravely maskt, their fancies may be told', and had declared: 'I can speake what I feele, and feele as much as they' (*Astrophil and Stella*, 3 and 6). Happily, neither Sidney nor Shakespeare consistently practise what their sonnet *personae* preach. No more can we assume that plainness of speech, or style, is the touchstone of sincerity. Plainness may itself become a convention, or an attitudinizing, as in some of Drayton's later sonnets (though it works supremely in 'Since there's no help', 1619 *Idea*, 61), and so self-defeating. Sidney can be as blatantly 'poetic' as any 'daintie wit'; but more characteristically he relies on a contrast of styles, achieving effects of immediacy by colloquial and 'dramatic' openings or by a sudden shock of homely directness at the end of an elaborate mythological conceit (as in 9,

---

[10] Cf. Joan Grundy, 'Shakespeare's Sonnets and the Elizabethan Sonneteers', *Shakespeare Survey* 15 (1962), pp. 41–9

'Queene *Vertue's* court . . . and poore I am their straw'; or in
17, 'His mother deare *Cupid* offended late, . . . and I was in his
way.') Above all, he prides himself with an almost exhibition-
ist joy on what he can make language do—not least when, as in
sonnet 35, he is at the very same time professing its impotence.
In this sonnet, the traditional notion that the lady beggars all
description—or, as Cassio describes Desdomona, 'excels the
quirks of blazoning pens' (*Othello*, II,i,63)—becomes the subject, or the excuse, of a gloriously confident exploration of
words, sweeping into its course a pun on Penelope Devereux/
Rich's name and ending with an implicit assertion of what
words may say when weighed and evaluated against themselves:

> What may words say, or what may words not say,
> Where truth it selfe must speake like flatterie?
> Within what bounds can one his liking stay,
> Where Nature doth with infinite agree?
>   What *Nestor's* counsell can my flames alay,
> Since Reason's selfe doth blow the cole in me?
> And ah what hope, that hope should once see day,
> Where *Cupid* is sworne page to Chastity?
> Honour is honour'd, that thou doest possesse
>   Him as thy slave, and now long needy Fame
>   Doth even grow rich, naming my *Stella's* name.
> Wit learnes in thee perfection to expresse,
>   Not thou by praise, but praise in thee is raisde:
>   It is a praise to praise, when thou art praisde.

Shakespeare's eloquence in the Time sonnets, or his ability to
perform wonders with plain, ordinary words in sonnets like
116, 'Let me not to the marriage of true minds', needs no
comment. His affirmation of 'true plain words' is part of a
more essentialist poetic—stated *and* enacted in his sonnets—than Sidney's. Sonnet 108, which—whatever the real
order of the sequence—looks back over much sonneteering,
encapsulates what he sees himself as doing in his verse:

What's in the brain that ink may character
Which hath not figur'd to thee my true spirit?
What's new to speak, what new to register,
That may express my love or thy dear merit?

Truly to 'express my love or thy dear merit' means to arrive at a oneness of subject and style—or, rather, to abandon 'style' (a word repeatedly associated with other, insincere, poets) altogether: 'In others' works thou dost but mend the style/. . . / But thou art all my art . . .' (78). His ultimate model is the plainest possible: all that is needed is to 'tell/That you are you' (84). But such a model is solipsistic; it reminds us that sincere expression may be an impossibility and every love poem disingenuous by definition. The sentiments of Dyer's best-known lines—

True hearts have ears and eyes, no tongues to speake.
They heare and see, and sigh, and then they breake—[11]

are echoed again and again by all the major sonneteers. Even Astrophil describes himself as approaching Stella 'Now with slow words, now with dumbe eloquence' (61). Hamlet the lover, we learn from the poem which Polonius reads out, went through the discovery that his art was inadequate to the beauty of his beloved and the truth of his feelings, and was reduced to a desperate literalness and double superlatives: 'O dear Ophelia, I am ill at these numbers. I have not art to reckon my groans; but that I love thee best, O most best, believe it' (II,ii, 119–20). Perhaps his most sincere moment in the play is that speechless one, reported by Ophelia in II,i, when—as in Dyer's lines—the only sound heard was 'a sigh so pietous and profound/As it did seem to shatter all his bulk/And end his being' (II,i, 94–6). No one would say that it is his finest moment, though; nor that we can be sure what his silence expressed: love, shock, horror, appeal for help? The silence of sincerity

[11] See Ralph M. Sargent, *At the Court of Queen Elizabeth: The Life and Lyrics of Sir Edward Dyer* (Oxford, 1935), p. 197 ('The Lowest Trees Have Tops').

may be effective in real life, and it may be effective in art when it is talked about, as by Astrophil, or in Viola's 'sister' who never told her love. It may even be effective in drama—as in the wonder of the reunion of Hermione and Leontes—if surrounded by speech and translated into a visual—stage—image. But ultimately the dramatic character must speak, and by definition the sonneteer must write.

We tend to feel that the reason why Sidney and Shakespeare in their sonnets affect us as they do—like men speaking to men[12]—is not because of their professions of sincerity but because they use the sonnet as a dramatic medium. The assumption, when we praise them above their fellow sonneteers because their verse 'rings true', or conveys 'the reality of passion', is that each has dramatized his true self (a self, needless to say, not limited to the lover of Penelope Rich, or the Fair Youth, or even Emilia Lanier). I wonder, though, if there are not some unexamined steps in such assumptions. The quotations at the head of my essay are intended to pinpoint a few of these.

II

Polonius's exhortation to Laertes, 'to thine own self be true', is the starting point of Lionel Trilling's fascinating book, *Sincerity and Authenticity*, in which he discusses the position of sincerity in the history of European thought and literature from the Renaissance onwards. The 'lucid moral lyricism' of Polonius's words, Trilling thinks, persuades us that, in conceiving of 'sincerity as an essential condition of virtue', he 'has had a moment of self-transcendence, of grace and truth' (p. 3). Certainly Polonius's lines appear out of tune with the rest of the speech of which they are a part—a curiously idealistic climax to a series of shrewd pieces of pragmatic paternal advice. But are they necessarily out of character? They can of course be played, in the theatre, as either *meant* or hypocritical

---

[12] Cf. Muir, *Shakespeare's Sonnets*, p. 29.

(or any shade between these two extremes), and anyone with experience of several *Hamlet* productions will have seen both. Within the text of *Hamlet* we have no evidence that Polonius is not motivated by a desire to be true to himself—as well as to Claudius, Ophelia, Hamlet and the rest. He is sincere when he proceeds, at once, to warn Ophelia against a lack of sincerity in Hamlet; though at the same time he proves the illogicality of his 'moral lyricism', for, while no doubt he is true to himself when he warns Ophelia, he is certainly false to Hamlet. He shows that narrowness of the moral imagination which makes it impossible for him to conceive of sincerity in others. Indeed this—apart from his prolixity—is the worst sin we can accuse him of as he sends Reynaldo to spy on Laertes and 'looses' Ophelia to Hamlet; and in the closet scene it becomes, ironically, fatal to him. The trouble with Polonius is that he does not see the complexities of his own maxim. But the play does, for it is in the nature of the dramatic medium that it asks us to look *around* the individual characters, and to judge them and their words by their context and their interaction with other characters. When Hamlet and Ophelia confront each other for the first time in the play, in the nunnery scene, who is sincere? The scene, intended by Polonius to reveal the sincere emotions of Hamlet, is ironically invalid as a test, for Hamlet is—though we cannot be sure how much—within his 'antic disposition', and Ophelia—who knows the frame-up—must also in some measure be acting. Within a few lines she is insincere (to put it politely) about her father's whereabouts and sincere in her lament for the 'noble mind here o'erthrown'. Hamlet sincerely believes that 'frailty, thy name is woman', but we cannot readily tell just how sincere, or otherwise, he is in his saying and unsaying of his love for Ophelia ('I loved you once' . . . 'I loved you not'). That Shakespeare intended this to remain a question is suggested by, if nothing else, the fact that he did not make it unmistakably clear just when Hamlet realizes that their interview is being overheard. It is part of the scene's effect, too, that it makes such different impacts on Polonius and Claudius, respectively. To Polonius it confirms the cause of Hamlet's behaviour as 'neglected love'; to the King it suggests neither love nor madness but something far more sinister. To us, finally—and this is of course the audience at which the dramatist aims—the scene as a whole speaks of the difficulties of knowing one's own self and the selves of others.

And that, I suppose, is also the ultimate effect of Polonius's lines—that is, when they are seen, or better still heard, within the full context of the dramatic fiction. Nor is the point altogether unrelated to the question of sincerity in the sonnet. Even as a dramatic monologue—even when, as often in Sidney and Shakespeare, it pretends to be one half of a dialogue—the sonnet obviously has not the drama's formal resources for exploring human relationships. It does not have the help of the actor's voice which by tempo and pitch and inflections, and silences, can speak that which is not written down and interpret that which is. It does not have the spectacle, even just of bodies in space; and it does not—even in as structured a sequence as *Astrophil and Stella*—form part of a developing action where each moment modifies every other. If these are limitations, Sidney takes full advantage of them: Astrophil remains in sole possession of the stage, with his courtly context as a background and Stella as a necessary sounding-board. His voice, unopposed and self-interpreted, with a *sprezzatura* that can convey both the seriousness and the absurdities of his passion, dominates the sequence; and it defines a self which remains the only realized self in the poems. The 'I' of Shakespeare's sonnets operates quite differently. His selflessness, as against Astrophil's self-absorption, has often been commented on; and so has the fact that Shakespeare often within each sonnet seems to aspire to the conditions of drama.[13] The point I wish to make is that the very sense of reality in the *Sonnets* is dramatic, while that in *Astrophil and Stella* is rhetorical: Sidney makes Astrophil persuade us that he

[13] See, e.g., G.K. Hunter, 'The Dramatic Technique of Shakespeare's Sonnets', *Essays in Criticism*, III (April, 1953), pp. 152–64; reprinted (like the Prince and Grundy essays referred to above) in the Macmillan *Casebook* volume on *The Sonnets*, ed. Peter Jones (London, 1977).

exists and feels what he says he feels; Shakespeare creates a
world (indeed, remembering the sonnets on Time, a universe)
in which the 'I' is capable of being radically changed and
developed by interaction with other selves. As a self, he is
amorphous and vulnerable.

To illustrate this point, I would refer to sonnet 42:

> That thou hast her, it is not all my grief,
> And yet it may be said I lov'd her dearly;
> That she hath thee is of my wailing chief,
> A loss in love that touches me more nearly.
> Loving offenders, thus I will excuse ye:
> Thou dost love her because thou know'st I love her,
> And for my sake even so doth she abuse me,
> Suff'ring my friend for my sake to approve her.
> If I lose thee, my loss is my love's gain,
> And, losing her, my friend hath found that loss;
> Both find each other, and I lose both twain,
> And both for my sake lay on me this cross.
>   But here's the joy: my friend and I are one;
>   Sweet flattery! then she loves but me alone.

It is not one of the more famous sonnets. It certainly uses 'true
plain words', and not a single 'Petrarchan' conceit. The only
conceit is the premiss 'that my friend and I are one', which is
brought in to solve the equation set up by the argument. The
ingenuity of the verbal game of loving, losing, and finding—structured towards a resolution with the inherent
inevitability of the sonnet form—might well lay this sonnet
open to accusations of insincerity. And yet, it soon becomes
apparent that the verbal game is played by the author much
like the disguise games in Shakespeare's comedies, to uncover
the real nature and feelings of the participants, including of
course the 'I'. The blunt, unexplained (because self-explained)
pronouns of the opening line tease us into imagining a dramatic situation, and the verbal paradoxes of the second and
third quatrains—e.g., 'If I lose thee, my loss is my love's

gain'—both outline and fill with contrary emotions our sense of the three-cornered relationship. Though the 'I' speaks, we are invited, by the stress and play on the pronouns, to see this from different viewpoints—those of each of the 'loving offenders' as well as the 'I'—and so we also see the 'I' as much from the outside as, ostentatiously with his 'thus I will excuse ye', he himself is trying *not* to. The very ingenuity of his excuse becomes a measure of how much he wants it to be true, to move from the 'grief' of the first line to the 'joy' of the thirteenth; the ambiguity of the 'sweet flattery' in the last line suggests that he both does and does not believe it. To us, the disguise reveals; by him it is sustained to the *apparently* triumphant ending: 'then she loves but me alone'. The poignancy of this sincere insincerity of the 'I', suspended between two kinds of love, might be compared with the self-assurance of the Sidney sonnet which I quoted earlier ('What may words say . . .'), to illustrate what I mean by Shakespeare's dramatic sense of reality, versus Sidney's rhetorical sense.

The 'I' of Shakespeare's sonnets—whether it is ingenuous (or apparently so) as in sonnet 42, or knowing as in sonnet 138 ('When my love swears that she is made of truth')—is not so much selfless as defined by interaction with other selves. Astrophil desires Stella, or grieves at losing her; the 'I' identifies himself with the object of his love, to the point where the sonnet clichés of exchanged hearts acquire the intensity of Cathy Earnshaw's 'Nelly, I *am* Heathcliff!' The self 'depends' (92) and 'belongs' (88), and it is dissolved and re-made in wonder at the very thought of the beloved (29). Only once does the 'I' make an assertion of a kind to suggest a simple and strong sense of self: 'I am that I am' (121)—my second headnote quotation. Dover Wilson, in his edition of the *Sonnets*, warns against making much of this statement for the wrong reasons—its verbal anticipation of Iago's 'I am not what I am', etc.—but I think one ought to make something of the fact that it *is* the only statement of its kind, and that it is uttered under provocation, by the 'I' having to defend himself against slanderers:

> I am that I am; and they that level
> At my abuses reckon up their own.

One ought, finally, to make something of its similarity, as a verbal model, to the definition of the sonnet poetic: 'to tell/That you are you'—words so true and plain as to have given up any other function than that of pointing to something beyond fiction (not only the fiction of slanderers) and beyond language.

If, then, the sincerity of Shakespeare's sonnets is an aspect of his keen and dramatically expressed sense of the difficulty of knowing and showing one's self, and if this sense manifests itself in an urge to move *through* fiction to a reality where 'you are you' and 'I am that I am', then Sidney presents an interesting contrast. Where Shakespeare involves us by the sense that he is going beyond fiction, Sidney dazzles and impresses us by the wholeness and self-containedness of his fiction. Hamlet's most virulent onslaught on himself ('O, what a rogue and peasant slave am I!') comes about through the realization that fiction may be truer—i.e. have a more effective emotional impact—than true life:

> Is it not monstrous that this player here,
> But in a fiction, in a dream of passion,
> Could force his soul so to his own conceit.
>
> (*Hamlet*, II,ii,544–6)

What is 'monstrous' to Hamlet, and a cause for self-castigation resolved only by his determination to test Claudius by another fiction, is to Astrophil a lesson learned and wittily absorbed. In sonnet 45, as Stella remains unmoved by the real thing—'the verie face of wo/Painted in my beclowded stormie face'—but weeps in pity at a fable of 'lovers never known', the logic of what to do is inevitable:

> Then thinke my deare, that you in me do reed
> Of Lover's ruine some sad Tragedie:
> I am not I, pitie the tale of me.

Though Stella both is and knows the cause of Astrophil's real-life misery, she shares with the narrator of Henry James's tale, 'The Real Thing', an 'innate preference for the represented subject over the real one: the defect of the real one was so apt to be a lack of representation'.[14] Not only is this, from within the fiction of Astrophil and Stella, rather a body-blow to any simple belief in sincerity and its efficacy (such as 'mute eloquence'); but it is also a self-reflection, characteristic of the art of this sonnet sequence, justifying and consolidating itself as a fiction—'the tale of me'.

III

If the emotional impetus to *Astrophil and Stella* came from Sidney's love of Lady Rich, the *energeia* of the poetry comes from his awareness of himself as a poet and the way he uses Astrophil to project this. In a well-known passage in the *Apology for Poetry* (the writing of which must have at least partly overlapped with the writing of the sonnets) Sidney deals with poetic sincerity and how it is realized:

> But truly many of such writings as come under the banner of unresistible love, if I were a mistress, would never persuade me they were in love; so coldly they apply fiery speeches, as men that had rather read lovers' writings . . . , than that in truth they feel those passions, which easily (as I think) may be betrayed by that same forcibleness or *energia* (as the Greeks call it) of the writer.[15]

Ringler points out that *energeia*, as discussed by Aristotle and by Puttenham in their treatment of elocution, refers not to the

---

[14] Henry James, *Selected Tales*, Penguin ed. (Harmondsworth, 1964), p. 50.

[15] *An Apology for Poetry*, ed. Geoffrey Shepherd (Edinburgh, 1965), pp. 137–8.

emotion felt by the writer but to the effect that the sense of the words, 'inwardly working a stirre to the mynde', has on the reader.[16] Shepherd notes that the term came to Sidney from Renaissance theorists, notably Scaliger, who had modified its sense and renamed it *efficacia*, and who used it to refer to the power of presenting the poetic subject matter clearly.[17] As Shepherd also notes, the same idea is present in Sidney's basic test of poetry:

> for any understanding knoweth the skill of the artificer standeth in that *Idea* or fore-conceit of the work, and not in the work itself.[18]

It is, I think, basic to an understanding of *Astrophil and Stella* that, to Sidney, the test of the poet lies not in the genuineness of his passion but in the clarity with which he apprehends his '*Idea* or fore-conceit'; and the test of the poetry lies not in the maker's sincerity but in the effect on the reader. What Astrophil sees, when he follows the Muse's advice to look in his heart, is that *Idea*, and, when he writes, Sidney makes sure that his eyes are firmly fixed on the reader. *Astrophil and Stella* is 'the tale of me' rendered to the reader with such self-consciousness of its own art as to make it, as a tale, more akin to *Lolita* than to *Clarissa*.

This is not to suggest that the sequence is to be read as metapoetry: what is remarkable about Sidney's achievement is the way the love story and the poetic self-consciousness are not only interwoven but interacting and deeply interdependent. In a sense, it all hinges on the connective 'and' in the first line of the first sonnet: 'Loving in truth, and faine in verse my love to show'. The following three lines manage to use the same rhetorical figure—the climax, or *gradatio*—both to project the hoped-for course of the courtship and to compress Sidney's theory of the function of poetry, as we know it from

[16] Ringler, *The Poems of Sir Philip Sidney*, p. 459.
[17] Shepherd, *op. cit.*, p. 226.
[18] *An Apology, ed. cit.*, p. 101.

the *Apology*, to delight, teach, and move to action:

> That the deare She might take some pleasure of my paine:
> Pleasure might cause her reade, reading might make her
>   know,
> Knowledge might pitie winne, and pitie grace obtaine.

The next seven lines vividly present the strangulating effect of attempts at purely literary imitation; in the twelfth line this effect is seen as uterine inertia, and in the fourteenth the sequence leaps into the world thanks to the shock-tactics of the Muse. In the early reaches of the sequence it might look as if the exposition of the past and present history of Astrophil's love merely alternates with literary criticism: the account of the gradual growth of his love in 2 is followed by the attack in 3 on the 'daintie wits'; 4 and 5 establish the sense of self-betrayal and the conflict between will and wit, beauty and virtue, which is to dominate more than half of the sequence; and 6 follows with an attack on conventional love poetry. Eight sonnets of love analysis follow, and then 15 resumes the criticism developed in 1, 3 and 6, of poets who mechanically imitate current fashions. Yet, this is not the layer-cake which it sounds like, for in each of the 'critical' sonnets the argument explores the conceit that Stella is both his subject and inspiration, the idea and the form of his poetry. And the eloquently and wittily 'trembling voice' (6) which analyses his love in the intervening sonnets never lets us forget that he is writing, and why:

> To make my selfe beleeve, that all is well,
> While with a feeling skill I paint my hell.
>
> (2)

Whether or not every single sonnet in *Astrophil and Stella* is in its proper place, there is clearly a careful overall plan to the sequence, and individual sonnets must be seen in relation to it. Thus, the (apparent) doubts about the efficacy of his writing (34) and of words (35) are a long way from the confidence of the opening sonnet: thirty-odd sonnets of inner turmoil and unachieved love have intervened to form a bulk of experience. Living and writing are inextricably intertwined: in 21 the poems themselves are part of the self-reproach over 'My young mind marde'; and in 19 his words, even as they come from his pen, 'Avise themselves that they are vainely spent'. While the opening sonnet envisaged a practical rhetorical purpose for his verse, by 34 he can contemplate a purely therapeutic value as well:

> Come let me write, 'And to what end?' To ease
> A burthned heart.

But he also turns to analysing the rhetorical effect, not only watching himself write but also watching her read, *and* himself listening to her reading.

There is no evidence that Sidney ever sent the sonnets to Penelope Rich. But, within the fiction of *Astrophil and Stella*, Astrophil obviously presents them to Stella, and she reads them (44) and even reads some out loud (57, 58). These three sonnets deal with the cathartic effect of turning 'real' experience into art. In 44 this means, ironically, that his rhetoric is not effective in the way he foresaw in sonnet 1, for the 'heav'nly nature' of the listener brings about a kind of translation of the poet's message, such

> That once come there, the sobs of mine annoyes
> Are metamorphosed straight to tunes of joyes.

In 45, as we saw earlier, he deals with the emotive power of fiction as against real life; later, in 57 and 58, this notion is taken up and fused with that of 44. In 57, his 'thorowest words, fit for woe's selfe to grone' and intended by him to pierce her soul 'with sharpnesse of the mone', become metamorphosed as she 'sings' them 'most sweetly . . ./With that faire breast making woe's darknesse cleare'. And in 58 he watches himself as an audience: Stella's 'sweet breath', her voice and face when

reading, cause even 'sad me' to experience 'those sad words'
with 'ravishing delight'. In the *Apology* Sidney writes of 'the
sweet violence of a tragedy' (Shepherd, ed., p. 118); here he
makes Astrophil both implicitly and explicitly remind us that
pain becomes pleasure when raw experience is translated into
art.

Meanwhile, in the plot of the poems, the soul-searchings of
the first fifty sonnets have turned into a more direct pursuit,
with Virtue and Love (as in 64) arguing for the possession of
Stella. This change coincides with Astrophil's taking a new
interest in his own verse as the spontaneous overflow of
powerful feelings and an accompanying interest in the limitations of his medium. Sonnet 50, unusually, opens with a direct
appeal to Stella,

> *Stella*, the fulnesse of my thoughts of thee
> Cannot be staid within my panting breast,
> But they do swell and struggle forth of me,
> Till that in words thy figure be exprest,

but the gap between feeling and expression immediately
forces itself upon him,

> And yet as soone as they so formed be,
> According to my Lord *Love's* owne behest:
> With sad eyes I their weake proportion see,
> To portrait that which in this world is best.

The two impulses are paradoxically poised,

> So that I cannot chuse but write my mind,
> And cannot chuse but put out what I write,

and, as he comes to strike out what he has written, the lines
themselves stop his 'fury' of destruction, 'Because their fore-
front bare sweet *Stella's* name'. Thus, as the lines turn on
themselves and we realize that the poem is as much about itself

(even its own paper and ink) as about Astrophil's emotions, artifice is being made out of sincerity, and *vice versa*. As if in an epitome of the sonnet sequence as a whole, the effect of a contact with the mind of a sincere poet/lover is firmly held within an awareness that, as Emerson put it in a diary note, 'there is no deeper dissembler than the sincerest man'.[19] Perhaps this is the very essence of Sidney's *sprezzatura*.

We are now in the part of the plot where Astrophil has some success as a suitor. In the First Song he still celebrates Stella as the first cause of his poetry, but we soon seem to approach a climax where fulfilled love would equal silence (69, 70), for 'Wise silence is best musicke unto blisse' (70). Perhaps if Penelope Rich had not refused to compromise herself in real life, such a refusal would still have had to be invented. As it is, Astrophil's limited amorous successes seem at first to produce a kind of complacency in his sense of himself as a poet. Compared to earlier, more searching explorations of language and poetic inspiration, sonnet 74, which celebrates Stella's kiss as the reason 'that with so smooth an ease/My thoughts I speake, and what I speake doth flow/In verse, and that my verse best wits doth please' seems simply clever; and so does the poetic blackmail of 81, where he can only be silent if kissed. But, as we begin to sense a dialogue going on between the lovers, the concern with poetry begins to take the form of an interest in words as speech. In the paean of joy at approaching Stella's house, in 85, speech 'which wit to wonder ties' is seen as a structuring and controlling complement to emotion; and the Fifth Song is a whole history of the place of speech in their courtship—and, as such, far more than the mere 'filler' which it has been called.[20] The structure of the song becomes an image of the power of words: a series of 'I said' clauses lists the attributes he used to bestow on her; it is followed by a series of 'I say' clauses naming her by a row of evils, from 'ungrateful' to 'witch' and 'devil'. Their love has reached a turning-point;

---

[19] Ralph Waldo Emerson, *The Journals and Miscellaneous Notebooks*, ed. A.W. Plumstead and H. Hayford (Cambridge, Mass., 1969), iii, 423.
[20] Cf. Ringler, *The Poems of Sir Philip Sidney*, 'Introduction', p. xlv.

refusal and revenge are adumbrated; and there is an extraordinary sense of the reality of the relationship and the identity of
the lady depending on the words in which they are created:

> But now that hope is lost, unkindnesse kils delight,
> Yet thought and speech do live, though metamorphosd
>   quite.

For a moment we glimpse some of the horror of Othello
calling Desdemona a whore, but *Astrophil and Stella* is not a
tragedy, and in the last stanza comes the reversal into a kind of
tragicomedy. The key-point is, again, the power of
Astrophil's poetry to transform pain into delight:

> You see what I can say: mend yet your froward mind,
> And such skill in my Muse you reconcil'd shall find,
> That all these cruell words your praises shall be proved.

By now it is obvious that the Songs offer a medium com-
plementary to that of the sonnets: one more flexible and
allowing the epigrammatic paradoxes and reversals of the
sonnets to be expanded and examined. It is not surprising,
therefore, that the chief turning-point in the plot—the account
of the meeting at which Astrophil *almost* comes to possess
Stella, only to meet with a conclusive (however reluctant)
rebuttal—is embodied in a song. The Eighth Song is particularly relevant to my theme because Sidney sees and presents
this crucial scene so much in terms of the impotence *and* the
power of language. The method of presentation is a combi-
nation of third-person narration with dialogue, and the action
is structured as a series of speech acts, with each reversal
marked by, as it were, a translation into another mode of
speech. The meeting begins in a wordless mutual solace at each
other's sight and a silent dialogue of 'hearts', reported by the
narrator. When Astrophil breaks the silence, we are told, 'Love
did set his lips asunder,/Thus to speake in love and wonder'.
At the climax of Astrophil's plea for 'pity', the narrator inter-

venes to tell us of the lover's intention to turn to what nowa-
days is called body-language:

> There his hands in their speech, faine
> Would have made tongue's language plaine;

but the lady's hands reply in a language 'all grace excelling',
which she then translates into a most effective verbal rhetoric;

> Then she spake; her speech was such,
> As not eares but hart did tuch.

Her eloquence, then, frustrates his desires, and she leaves him

> so passion rent,
> With what she had done and spoken,
> That therewith my song is broken.

As in sonnet 50, the poem turns back on itself, but with more
poignancy than cleverness. The shock of this intrusion of the
first person possessive pronoun and the present tense in the last
line—the revision of viewpoints which it asks for—is something like that when we realize that the narrator of Camus's
The Plague is Rieux himself.

At this stage in the sequence, as declared lovers meet and the
lady is for once allowed a speech in her own voice, there is no
need to question either love or poetry, only the power of
speech. The Ninth Song, which follows immediately, uses the
pastoral convention as a distancing fiction to help Astrophil
bear the unbearable, though the translation into pastoral is
deliberately (it would seem) made so thin that the 'real' situation shows through the idiom, as Astrophil dismisses his
flock to seek shelter from the 'stormes' in his heart and the
'showers' of his tears. The most interesting use of the convention is to point the absolute nadir of the lover's feelings and the
poet's art which can now operate only by proxy and as sub-
human utterance. He abandons his sheep, asking them, if they

should meet with Stella, to 'Tell her in your piteous blay-ing,/Her poore slave's unjust decaying'.

As the moment of intimacy and confrontation, enacted in the Eighth Song, recedes into the past (its mixed impulses of grief and joy analysed in the oxymorons of sonnet 87), the final section of the sequence deals with Astrophil's despair, his sorrow at Stella's absence, and his attempts to establish some kind of emotional existence without her. There is one return, in sonnet 90, to discussing his verse and its purpose, curiously out of place here and harking back to the very first sonnet in its untroubled affirmation of Stella as subject, inspiration and technique. Sonnet 104 hits out at the 'envious wits' who grudge him 'my sorrowe's eloquence'. But when that elo-quence contemplates itself, it does so only in terms of the difficulty of finding an adequate language for grief. It is inter-esting to find that the most 'felt' evocation of his state of mind is in a sonnet (94) not about grief as such but about the difficulty of writing about grief when you feel it. The first four lines take us right into the desperate gropings for the '*Idea* or fore-conceit' in a mind where introspection can no longer trace the curve of the feeling:

> Griefe find the words, for thou hast made my braine
>   So darke with misty vapors, which arise
>   From out thy heavy mould, that inbent eyes
> Can scarce discerne the shape of mine owne paine.

'Looke in thy heart and write' is no longer the simple process it was. It would be easy to say that sonnet 94 is more sincere than sonnet 90; but it would also be misleading, if it suggested a kind of schizophrenia in the sequence as a whole. Sonnet 94 is, in its unrelieved pain, untypical; and even there the self-pity is partly purged by a verbal wit which plays with the personifica-tion of grief:

> though in wretchednesse thy life doth lie,
> Yet growest more wretched then thy nature beares,
> By being placed in such a wretch as I.

Already in the Tenth Song (placed between 92 and 93), some
joy had been wrought out of the exercise of imagining a future
meeting with Stella. The fiction is now that he is not writing,
merely thinking; the meeting is inarticulate ('Dovelike mur-
murings' and 'glad moning' are all the sounds) and indescrib-
able,

> Let no tongue aspire to tell,
> In what high joyes I shall dwell,

and the joy experienced is that of an erotic dream ('Thy
delights my woes increase,/My life melts with too much
thinking;/Thinke no more but die in me'). The escapism of
this joy is not repeated; by sonnet 100 ('O teares, no teares, but
raine from beautie's skies'), which I referred to at the beginning of this essay, we return to the cathartic theme, sounded
earlier in the sequence, of art turning sorrow itself into a thing
of beauty, and so of joy:

> O plaints conserv'd in such a sugred phraise,
> That eloquence it selfe envies your praise,
> While sobd out words a perfect Musike give.
> Such teares, sighs, plaints, no sorrow is, but joy.

For the neatness of my theme—that the sequence as a whole
not only speaks of, but also enacts, the power of poetry to turn
a brazen and painful world into a golden and delightful one—it
would have been better if sonnet 100 had also been the last,
rounding off a perfect Hecatompathia. But it is not, and no
doubt it is truer to the contrary impulses which the sequence is
also about that it goes on, from this moment of aesthetic *stasis*,
to say and unsay consolation through eight more sonnets and
one Song. The Eleventh Song makes a dialogue out of just that

pattern, lover and beloved sharing each stanza, she proffering two lines of resignation, consolation, and possible compensation, he answering with three dialectically opposed lines. The symmetrical pattern keeps the scene to one of sweet nostalgia rather than turbulent emotion. But then, as if to give the whole sequence the kind of twist which Drayton provides in the couplet of his 'Since there's no help', the last four sonnets bring the agony of grief back; and the last sonnet ends on a balance of two unresolved paradoxes. So strange is her effect on him

> That in my woes for thee thou art my joy,
> And in my joyes for thee my only annoy.

It was Nashe who, in the preface to the unauthorized edition of 1591, described *Astrophil and Stella* as a 'tragicommody of love'.[21] The modern editor of the sonnets thinks that the action is tragic (Ringler, p. xlix). But from the point of view of the reader, the tragedy is made 'sweet' by the poetry in which it is presented. And that is the viewpoint which individual sonnets, and the structure of the sequence as a whole, has been pressing upon us. If Sidney is dramatic, he is also the dramatic critic who interprets the dramatic work for us. Or, to put it another way, if Sidney is dramatizing his material, what he is dramatizing is not only a love story, nor only an anatomy of self, but also a critical theory. This does not mean that he wishes to dull our responses to 'actual' feelings. On the contrary, he wishes

---

[21] Nashe's description translates the sequence into 'this Theater of pleasure' by using terms which are clearly often derived from the poems themselves: 'for here you shal finde a paper stage streud with pearle . . . whiles the tragicommody of love is performed by starlight. The chiefe actor here is *Melpomene*, whose dusky robes dipt in the ynke of teares . . . The argument cruell chastitie, the Prologue hope, the Epilogue dispaire.' (*The Complete Works of Sir Philip Sidney*, ed. A. Feuillerat, (London, 1922), II, p. 369).

to alert and extend them: to make us feel not only that he is a sincere man, speaking to men, but that he is a sincere poet—one who knows that life is larger than the individual experience and that art is truer than life.

John Donne's Newsless Letters

JOHN CAREY

DONNE'S letters abound with problems for editors and annotators, and they also present something of a stumbling block for the common reader since they are, by and large, extremely dull—indeed, perversely and elaborately dull in a way which, we feel, the letters of a great poet have no right to be. This essay will try to disperse some of that dullness by suggesting that it was intended by Donne as a highly specialized and functional sort of dullness, based on imaginative theories which tie in closely with his poems.

About two hundred of Donne's letters survive[1] (it is not possible to be more precise than that because some surviving letters are only dubiously attributable to him). The majority were collected by his son, the unamiable John Donne D.C.L., and published in two volumes, *Letters to Severall Persons of Honour*, 1651 (here referred to as *Letters*), and *A Collection of Letters, Made by Sr Tobie Mathews Kt.*, 1660. Broadly, the difference between the two collections is that the first contains letters to close friends, while in the second the letters are more formal and addressed to elevated persons such as the Earl of Somerset and the Queen of Bohemia. This makes the first collection more intriguing for us, but for John Donne D.C.L. the contrary was true. He saw snob-appeal as an incentive to buyers, and so tried to disguise the relatively private nature of the first collection by concealing actual addressees and substituting names or initials with grander associations. This

---

[1] See *A Bibliography of Dr John Donne*, ed. Sir Geoffrey Keynes, 4th edition, Oxford, 1973, pp. 133–59, which lists all known and attributed Donne letters.

fraud went undetected until Professors Shapiro and Bennett investigated it in the mid-twentieth century and reallocated the letters to their rightful correspondents.[2] The prime purpose behind the fraud, it emerged, had been to conceal the fact that over half the letters in the volume were actually addressed to Donne's loyal and generous friend Sir Henry Goodyer—a forgotten name by 1651, with no market value.

Various other letters, uncollected by Donne's son, have come to light over the years, the largest cache being a group of thirty-two letters from manuscripts at Burley-on-the-Hill, published by Evelyn Simpson in 1924. Some of these, however, are arguably not by Donne at all.[3] Even if we discount the doubtful items, the body of Donne's correspondence is uniquely large for his period—the first sizeable collection of letters by an English poet to survive. That makes their uninformative character the more galling. True, they have their vivid flashes, which we all remember: the letter written to Goodyer 'from the fireside in my parlour, and in the noise of three gamesome children', or the letter to the same correspondent written after a worried, wakeful night, during which Mrs Donne gave birth to a son.[4] But these are untypical. Donne, in his letters, mentions his family rarely and his poems almost never. The rich interest in art and literature which Keats and Byron show us in their correspondence is totally absent from Donne's. These omissions must disappoint us, but they should not take us entirely by surprise. For the extant letters were almost all written to courtiers, and Donne was anxious that they should not associate him with anything as low as family matters or poetry.

More curious than this avoidance of private and literary

[2] I.A. Shapiro, 'The Text of Donne's *Letters to Severall Persons*', *RES*, vii, 291–301; Roger E. Bennett, 'Donne's Letters from the Continent in 1611-12', *PQ*, xix (1940), 66–78, and Donne's *Letters to Severall Persons of Honour*', *PMLA*, lvi (1941), 120–40.

[3] Evelyn Simpson, *A Study of the Prose Works of John Donne*, 2nd edition, 1948, pp. 291–336. For the dispute about attribution see Keynes, *Bibliography*, pp. 157–8.

[4] *Letters*, pp. 137 and 146–7.

topics is the tendency of Donne's letters to contain no subject matter at all. This aspect has not escaped the notice of the few modern critics who have bothered to discuss them. 'One wonders,' writes E. N. S. Thompson, 'why Donne's letters are so destitute of real news, and what his correspondents derived from them to justify the pains the sender was put to.'[5] Donne, observes W.H. Irving, seems unable to say anything 'simply and directly' in his letters. The 'vast intertwinings of the phrases would make most of us wonder whether his friend really understood what he was trying to say.'[6] A third critic, Mrs Simpson, misses in Donne's letters 'the delightfully intimate outpourings on every possible subject, grave or gay' which she finds in Walpole, Cowper and Lamb, and concludes that Donne's prose style was 'ill suited for familiar correspondence'.[7]

Criticism, we feel, ought to be able to do better than this. Yet these complaints are justified, so far as they go. Not, we must observe, that they do justice to the variety of Donne's correspondence. For Donne basically wrote two types of letters—one with news and one without. As an instance of the first type we might take the letter to Goodyer advising him that the King had appointed nine of the Council to negotiate with the Spanish ambassador.[8] Stuffed with court and foreign doings this could by no stretch of the imagination be judged 'destitute of real news', and it transmits its concerns in a quite straightforward style. Equally circumstantial is his letter to Mrs Cockain giving details of his health—one of Donne's permanent preoccupations.[9] What we learn from such examples is that the vacuous 'intertwinings' of other letters must, whatever their motive, represent a deliberate choice—for Donne, when he wishes, could be as chatty and

---

[5] E.N.S. Thompson, *Literary Bypaths of the Renaissance*, New Haven, 1924, pp. 111–12.
[6] W.H. Irving, *The Providence of Wit in the English Letter Writers*, Durham, N. Carolina, 1955, p. 91.
[7] Simpson, *Prose Works*, p. 292.
[8] *Letters*, pp. 82–4. For similar newsy letters, see pp. 42, 154–9, 165–7.
[9] *A Collection of Letters, Made by Sr Tobie Mathews Kt.*, 1660, p. 341.

topical as anyone else.

Donne was evidently well aware that his letters at times lacked any substance, and this unconventional quality caused him some qualms. 'No mans Letters might be better wanted than mine', he admits, 'since my whole Letter is nothing else but a confession that I should and would write.'[10] Sometimes he excuses himself by urging that there is simply no news to be had in his present location: 'I can from hence requite you with no news which hath made me fill paper with the vanyty of myne owne discourse.' Sufficiently elaborated, this excuse can itself provide something to write about:

> Sir, I would some great princes or men were dead so I might chuse them or some states or Countryes overthrowne so I were not in them that I might have some newes to ease this itch of writing which travayles me.[11]

Donne's compulsion to make contact with another human being through letters was, we gather from this, quite independent of any useful or interesting matter he had to convey.

Donne's protestations about his newsless environment may, to some degree, be taken at face value. When he was living at Mitcham, after his marriage, and writing as his practice was each Tuesday to Goodyer, he may well have felt that the past week had not yielded anything momentous enough to divert his friend at court. The oddly empty type of letter he evolved may, originally, have been a response to this difficult situation. Though the dating of Donne's letters presents problems, it seems clear that a number of the newsless variety do belong to the Mitcham period.

But the explanation that Donne was not in a position to supply his correspondents with solid intelligence cannot in itself account for the sort of letters he sent. For one thing, he continues to protest about a local lack of news even on foreign travels when, we feel, almost anyone else would have found

---

[10] *Letters*, p. 87.
[11] Simpson, *Prose Works*, pp. 308, 312–13.

something novel to communicate. Writing to George Gerrard
from Spa in July 1612, for instance, he deplores 'the peremp-
tory barrennesse of this place, from whence we can write
nothing into *England*, but of that which comes from thence'.[12]
That remark does not suggest either a very eager pursuit of
local curiosities, or a ready understanding of the extent to
which foreign scenes and manners, however mundane, can
entertain readers back home.

The fact is, I believe, that Donne's evasions and excuses
about the supply of news conceal a quite deep-rooted unwillingness to contaminate his letters with news or gossip at all.
He realized that normal usage required him to give his correspondents something newsy to bite on, but he resented this
obligation because it interfered with the introspective concentration which he liked to cultivate. News of a general
nature struck him as an intrusion upon a letter's proper privacy. Letters were thus, for Donne, akin to meditations. Gener-
ally when writing to Goodyer he composed the letter either in
his library ('where to cast mine eye upon good Authors kin-
dles or refreshes sometimes meditations not unfit to communicate to near friends'), or else he let his mind dwell on it
and gradually formulate it while he was riding along the
highway ('where I am contracted, and inverted into
myself').[13] That it should not occur to Donne to look at the
landscape or the passers-by while travelling is entirely typical
of his almost pathological self-absorption.

The idea that Donne deliberately emptied his letters of
matter is supported by a letter to an unknown correspondent,
first printed by Gosse, in which he apologises for including
news of other people at all, and implies that to do so is vulgar,
promiscuous and desultory. After passing on a few scraps of
gossip ('My Lord of Bedford, I hear, had lately a desperate fall
from his horse . . . his lady rode away hastily from Twick-
enham to him'), he pulls himself up sharply:

[12] *Letters*, p. 92.
[13] *Letters*, p. 137.

> And thus long, Sir, whilst I have been talking to others, methinks I have opened a casement to gaze upon passengers which I love not much, though it might seem a recreation to such as who have their houses, that is themselves, so narrow and ill furnished, yct I can be content to look inward upon myself, if for no other object, yet because I find your name and fortune and contentment in the best room of me.[14]

The implication that to let his mind wander to anyone else would be a sign of empty-headedness, and the accompanying suggestion that self-examination provides the most intimate communion with his correspondent, are both pointers which help us to locate Donne's deeper convictions about letter-writing. The letter just quoted was sent, we should notice, from Mitcham ('my Hospital')—and this reinforces our sense that the newslessness of the Mitcham letters cannot, in the last resort, be attributed to the fact that the place was remote from any notable goings-on. Even when he had news to dispatch from Mitcham, Donne, we see, was liable to feel the inclusion of it in a letter to be somehow reprehensible.

The notion that a letter is, or should ideally be, too private a receptacle to permit mention of third parties, helps to explain why Donne, on occasion, relegates the only piece of news which his letter contains to a postscript. An example of this occurs in the third of his extant letters to Bridget White, Lady Kingsmill, which is worth quoting since it illustrates in a fairly extreme form the amount of emptiness which Donne could get into a letter when he tried:

> Madame. I have but small comfort in this letter; the messenger comes too easily to me, and I am too sure that the letter shall be delivered. All adventures towards you should be of more difficulty and hazard. But perchance I need not lament this; it may be so many of my letters are lost already that it is time that one should come, like *Jobs* servant, to bring word, that the rest were lost. If you have had more

---

[14] Edmund Gosse, *The Life and Letters of John Donne*, 1899, ii, 16.

before, this comes to aske how they were received; and if you have had none, it comes to try how they should have been received. It comes to you like a bashful servant, who though he have an extreme desire to put himself in your presence, yet hath not much to say when he is come: yet hath it as much to say as you can think; because what degrees so ever of honour, respect, and devotion, you can imagine or beleeve to be in any, this letter tells you, that all those are in me towards you. So that for this letter you are my Secretary; for your worthinesses, and your opinion that I have a just estimation of them, write it: so that it is as long, and as good, as you think it; and nothing is left to me, but as a witness, to subscribe the name of

Your most humble servant
J.D.

Though this letter be yours, it will not misbecome or disproportion it that I mention your Noble brother, who is gone to *Cleave*, not to return till towards Christmas, except the business deserve him not so long.[15]

From a strictly utilitarian point of view, this letter has nothing to offer its recipient beyond its postscript. Admittedly, its vacuous air is not quite so purposeless as might at first appear. Its first four sentences are evidently designed to inquire, in the most deferential and unimportunate way, why Donne has received no acknowledgement of his previous letters. But apart from that the letter is not so much empty as non-existent. It nominates Bridget White herself as the letter-writer, and whatever she can imagine or believe will, he tells her, be the letter's substance. It adapts itself precisely to its recipient's state of mind, but it does so at the expense of its own identity. The recipient's state of mind will determine its form and content.

This delegation of authorial responsibility appealed to Donne, as we shall see, in his correspondence with Goodyer

---

[15] *Letters*, pp. 5–6. For another example of a postscript containing a letter's news see *Letters*, pp. 48–52.

also. It helped him in his imaginative desire to transform a letter into its recipient. He can tell Bridget White that the letter is hers in a double sense, for it is by her as well as to her. It becomes a piece of her mind, in Donne's keeping. It joins their two thoughts, because they compose it jointly. As Donne writes he is aware that Bridget will, in reading, write again, and differently, what he has written.

Letter-writing in the Renaissance was, like most other activities, surrounded by a body of theory, and it naturally occurs to us to ask, before going any further, whether the tendency towards functional emptiness which we seem to be finding in Donne's letters can be explained by reference to any of the classical models commonly recommended at the time, or to the popular manuals of epistolary instruction. The answer, in both cases, is a distinct negative. The two chief models were, of course, Cicero and Seneca. Cicero's letters, unlike Donne's, are packed with news, gossip and family matters, providing the raw material for a history of his time. Languet advised Sidney to mould his letters on Cicero's because of the 'important matters they contain', adding that 'there is nowhere a better statement of the causes which overthrew the Roman Republic'.[16] Seneca's letters, on the other hand, resemble moral essays, and take Cicero's to task for dwelling on everyday affairs. That might suggest some kinship between Seneca and Donne, especially as Donne's newsless letters to Goodyer repeatedly take the form of general discourses upon such topics as friendship, the soul, and court and country life.[17] But in fact the dissimilarities are marked. Seneca's letters are far more pointed, purposeful and assertive, and his clear Stoic principles belong to a different world from Donne's ruminative rambles.

In a letter to Goodyer about letter-writing[18] Donne expressly segregates himself from both these classical models.

[16] *The Correspondence of Sir Philip Sidney and Hubert Languet*, ed. and trans. Steuart A. Pears, 1845, pp. 19–20.
[17] See, for example, *Letters*, pp. 42–8, 61–4, 70–3.
[18] *Letters*, pp. 105–8.

He starts by praising the letter as a form ('No other kinde of conveyance is better for knowledge, or love'), and goes on to celebrate an array of ancient and modern letter-writers, who have contributed to the sum of human knowledge ('What treasures of Morall knowledge are in *Senecaes* Letters to onely one *Lucilius*? . . . how much of the storie of the time, is in *Ciceroes* Letters?'). But his own letters, he explains, are not intended to be instructive like these: 'it is the other capacity which must make mine acceptable, that they are also the best conveyors of love.' They may, he concedes, contain knowledge as well, but it will be living knowledge, not the sort you find 'buried in Books'. Having given himself this build-up he might, he realizes, be expected to produce a piece of living knowledge. Instead he laughingly climbs down: 'Since then at this time, I am upon the stage, you may be content to hear me. And now that perchance I have brought you to it . . . I have nothing to say. And it is well, for the Letter is already long enough.' The joke, like all jokes, gives a feeling of personal warmth and closeness, and that seems to be Donne's intent. He communicates living knowledge while declaring his inability to supply any. He avoids the slab of cold fact which lies between any informer and his informant, and he does so by keeping subject matter at arm's length.

There is no precedent then for Donne's epistolary methods in Cicero or Seneca. The letter-writing manuals of his day are equally remote from the sophisticated uses to which he puts the form. The two in widest circulation were William Fulwood's *The Enemie of Idlenesse*, 1568, and Angel Day's *The English Secretorie*, 1586. Fulwood divides letters into three categories (Doctrine, Mirth, Gravity) and every letter into three parts (cause, intent, consequence). The letters he describes and exemplifies nearly all have a distinct aim (comforting a friend on the death of his son; asking advice from an advocate, etc.). He realizes that his readers might sometimes want to write letters without any such express purpose, and he includes an appropriate section ('How to visit our Frend with Letters, not having any great matter to write').

However, here too he sticks to his tripartite structure. After a frank beginning—'Although I have no mater to write unto you (my deare friend). . .'—the letter should, he advises, consist of a declaration of love, a report on the writer's health, and a request for letters from the correspondent.[19]

The barren schematization endemic to literary thought in the Renaissance is even more apparent in Angel Day. He gives four kinds of letters (Demonstrative, Deliberative, Judicial and Familiar), and further divides familiar letters into Narratory (telling of our present affairs), Nuntiatory (carrying news), Gratulatory, Remuneratory, Collaudatory (recommending someone to preferment), Jocatory (containing a joke), Prestolatory (tendering our services to someone) and Objurgatory (rebuking ill demeanour). However, apart from offering this classification Day never gets round to discussing familiar letters at all, as he devotes his book to the treatment of Demonstrative letters (describing a thing or person) and Deliberative letters (entailing persuasion, recommendation or consolation). Whether anyone, in practice, learnt anything from Fulwood or Day seems doubtful, and that Donne did not is certain.

Whatever else we may think of Donne's letters, a comparison of them with the models his culture made available only reinforces our impression of his originality. His omission of subject matter is an index of his greater seriousness, vis-a-vis Fulwood or Day, rather than the reverse. Letters had, for him, a kind of holiness. He calls them 'frendships sacraments',[20] and suggests that the action of writing them is a spiritual exercise. That it should take place at all is more important than the question of whether the letters ever arrive at their destination. It is, like prayer, self-justifying. He explains this in a letter to Goodyer:

---

[19] William Fulwood, *The Enemie of Idlenesse*, 1568, pp. 72–3. On Fulwood and his successors see Jean Robertson, *The Art of Letter Writing*, Liverpool, 1942, and Katherine Gee Hornbeak, *The Complete Letter-Writer in English, 1568-1800*, Smith College Studies in Modern Language, xv, 3–4, April–July 1934, to which Robertson seems much indebted.

[20] Simpson, *Prose Works*, p. 311.

I make account that this writing of letters, when it is with
any seriousness, is a kind of extasie, and a departure and
secession and suspension of the soul, which doth then
communicate it self to two bodies: And as I would every
day provide for my souls last convoy, though I know not
when I shall die, and perchance I shall never die; so for these
extasies in letters, I oftentimes deliver my self over in writing when I know not when those letters shall be sent to you,
and many times they never are, for I have a little satisfaction
in seeing a letter written to you upon my table, though I
meet no opportunity of sending it.[21]

This is a key paragraph for understanding the kind of letter
Donne writes, and its mention of ecstasy obviously directs our
attention to links between the letters and the poems. If letters
are ecstasies, then the absence of news and the exclusion of
other kinds of impersonal subject matter becomes no more
than what is expected. For from the meeting of souls all
temporal and external features must naturally be excluded.
The insecurity or arrogance (or both) which made Donne
spurn the outer world and its doings is familiar to us from 'The
Sunne Rising':

> Goe tell Court-huntsmen, that the King will ride,
> Call countrey ants to harvest offices;
> Love, all alike, no season knowes, nor clyme,
> Nor houres, dayes, moneths, which are the rags of time.

'The Canonization' voices the same contempt for mundane
affairs:

> With wealth your state, your minde with Arts improve,
> Take you a course, get you a place,
> Observe his honour, or his grace,
> Or the Kings reall, or his stamped face
> Contemplate, what you will, approve,
> So you will let me love.

[21] *Letters*, p. 11 (for the addressee see R.E. Bennett, *PMLA*, lvi (1941), 134,
and *PQ*, xix (1940), 75).

The need for a secluded and uncontaminated space, a 'little room', in which love may surmount worldly concerns, is imaginatively met by such poems, and it is the same need that prompts Donne to experiment with a new kind of letter, devoid of anything as earth-bound as subject matter. The relegation of news items to a postscript, leaving the body of the letter pure and empty, is only a more pointed version of the same endeavour.

The exclusion of news serves to make letters timeless, so that they may partake of the spirit rather than the body. In the poems the timelessness of love is invoked with the specific purpose of extricating it from those areas of experience which usually generate news items:

> All Kings, and all their favorites,
> All glory of honors, beauties, wits,
> The Sun it selfe, which makes times, as they passe,
> Is elder by a yeare now, then it was
> When thou and I first one another saw:
> All other things, to their destruction draw,
>   Only our love hath no decay;
> This, no to morrow hath, nor yesterday . . .
> ('The Anniversarie', 1–8)

So, too, in letters either to close friends or to those with whom he wishes to cultivate closeness, Donne expressly avoids features that suggest temporality. 'In the offices of so spirituall a thing as friendship', he tells George Gerrard, 'so momentary a thing as time must have no consideration'[22] —and he concludes that it is unnecessary to put dates on one's letters. He makes the same point in a letter to the Countess of Bedford:

for though in inheritances and worldly possessions we consider the dates of Evidencces, yet in Letters, by which we deliver over our affections, and assurances of friendship, and the best faculties of our souls, times and dates cannot

[22] *Letters*, p. 246.

have interest, nor be considerable, because that which passes by them, is eternall, and out of the measure of time.[23]

Since, by this argument, time and temporal events must be regarded as a debasement in letters, we find Donne disparaging those of his letters which contain items of news by comparison with those which have nothing whatsoever to relate. At the start of a lengthy letter to Goodyer about doings at court, and the possibility of his own advancement to a secretaryship in Ireland, he explains that he stoops to this topical subject matter only because he is pretty sure the letter will not reach its destination: 'this Letter shall but talke, not discourse; it shall but gossip, not consider, not consult, so it is made halfe with a prejudice of being lost by the way'.[24]

Cynical readers may doubt the sincerity of these protestations. Is not Donne simply flattering his influential acquaintances by assuring them that his regard for them transcends time and worldly considerations? Should we not discount his pretence, in the letter to Goodyer, that he ventures to mention his desire for a secretaryship solely because he expects the letter to get lost? Isn't it patently a ruse, concealing his ambition (which, as we know, was desperately intense) behind an affectation of courtly nonchalance? A tentative yes is probably the right answer to all these questions. But it would be naive to assume that this renders Donne's world-scorning postures insincere. It was necessary for him to persuade himself that his friendships were not mercenary, and that his personal integrity had survived the failure of his career. We detect the same pressure behind his love poems. It is not because Donne is, in any simple sense, indifferent to kings, favourites and court honours that, in 'The Anniversarie' or 'The Canonization', he registers his superiority to them so stridently. By the same token, the high-minded exclusion of newsworthy items from some letters is perfectly compatible with the eager communication of court gossip in others. Both types of letter testify, in

23 *Letters*, p. 22–3.
24 *Letters*, p. 143.

their different ways, to the same anxiety about his position
vis-a-vis the great world.

Of course, writing letters without any substance presented a
practical problem. However firmly Donne believed that
letter-writing, when seriously undertaken, amounted to 'a
kind of extasie', and however sincerely he assured Sir Henry
Wotton that 'more then kisses, letters mingle Soules',[25] the fact
remained that the soul conveyed by the letter had to be
embodied in something. Compared to kisses, letters were at a
disadvantage in having to be verbal. To rid them wholly of
substance was to annihilate them. Donne realized this the
more keenly because the relation of soul to body was to him a
perpetual problem. In 'The Extasie', as elsewhere, he reminds
us of the soul's dependence on the body. Bodies bring souls
together.

> On man heavens influence workes not so,
> But that it first imprints the ayre,
> Soe soule into the soule may flow,
> Though it to body first repaire.

So letters must have some body, if only a body of 'ayre', as
Donne tells Goodyer in a letter about letters:

> You know that for aire we are sure we apprehend and enjoy
> it, but when this air is rarified into fire, we begin to dispute
> whether it be an element, or no: so when Letters have a
> convenient handsome body of news, they are Letters; but
> when they are spun out of nothing, they are nothing, or but
> apparitions, and ghosts, with such hollow sounds, as he that
> hears them, knows not what they said. You (I think) and I
> am much of one sect in the Philosophy of love; which
> though it be directed upon the minde, doth inhere in the
> body, and find prety entertainment there: so have Letters
> for their principall office, to be seals and testimonies of
> mutuall affection, but the materialls and fuell of them

[25] John Donne, *The Satires, Epigrams and Verse Letters*, ed. W. Milgate,
Oxford, 1967, p. 71.

should be a confident and mutuall communicating of those things which we know. How shall I then who know nothing write Letters? Sir, I learn knowledge enough out of yours to me. I learn that there is truth and firmnesse and earnestness of doing good alive in the world . . .[26]

The drift of Donne's thought here is close to that in 'The Extasie', and the conversations with Goodyer about the 'Philosophy of love', to which he seems to allude, belonged, we may conjecture, to the generative process behind that poem. The airy body of news which he deems necessary for letters plainly relates also to the angel in 'Aire and Angells' who must take 'face, and wings Of aire' in order to materialize. Love cannot inhere in 'nothing' (says 'Aire and Angells'), and according to Donne's letter it cannot inhere in letters 'spun out of nothing' either. Donne's endless puzzling over nothingness, materiality, and the entities that lie between them—souls, ghosts, angels—directs his imagination not only, we realize, in his poems and sermons but also when he is theorizing about, and writing, letters.

Another image from 'The Extasie' recurs in a letter Donne wrote to George Gerrard from Amiens, where he asserts, once more, the inferior status of news in letters. Having called himself Gerrard's 'friend', Donne writes:

if you will but write that you give me leave to keep that name still, it shall be the gold of your letter: and for alloy, put in as much newes as you will. We are in a place where scarce any money appeares, but base: as, I confesse, all matters of Letters is in respect of the testimonies of friendship.[27]

The friendship which letters testify to is superior to news as gold is to alloy. Yet if we gloss Donne's letter by reference to his poem we must remind ourselves that alloy is necessary to

[26] *Letters*, pp. 120–1.
[27] *Letters*, pp. 264–5.

make gold current, as bodies are necessary to allow the soul external expression. Bodies are not 'drosse to us, but allay', say the souls in 'The Extasie'.

The Gerrard letter, placed beside that to Goodyer about airy bodies, makes Donne's predicament plain. It is 'base' for letters to contain 'matters'. If they do so, they are no longer pure 'gold'. Yet if they do not, they are 'nothing'. Donne would not be Donne if he did not feel divided on the issue. It was his nature to perceive quandaries. So, in opposition to 'The Extasie', we find in 'A Valediction: forbidding Mourning' that souls do not need bodies after all—and in this poem the images of air and gold which Donne had employed to argue for the body's utility, are rearranged to prove the opposite case:

> Our two soules therefore, which are one,
>   Though I must goe, endure not yet
> A breach, but an expansion,
>   Like gold to ayery thinnesse beate.

Whether souls need bodies, and whether letters need a 'body of news', are, then, closely connected questions in Donne's mind, suggesting the same images and prompting the same vacillation. One factor which inclined him to favour newsless letters was his habitual fascination with the idea of the essence, which outshines and renders superfluous a mass of surrounding matter. Applied to letters, this reductive impulse produced a theory of the letter as condensed replica of its sender—a miniature surrogate person, as it were, like the scrawled signature on the pane of glass in 'A Valediction: of my Name in the window'. A corollary of this theory was that a letter should have no specific purpose—for specificity would bind it to extraneous and ephemeral situations, instead of allowing it to be responsive and accommodating, like a living person. Donne tries out this idea on Goodyer in a letter which bears some resemblance to his poem 'Negative Love':

I send not my letters as a tribute, nor interest, nor recompense, nor for commerce, nor as testimonials of my love, nor provokers of yours, nor to justifie my custome of writing, nor for a vent and utterance of my meditations; for my Letters are either above or under all such offices; yet I write very affectionately, and I chide and accuse myself of diminishing that affection which sends them, when I ask my self why: onely I am sure that I desire that you might have in your hands Letters of mine of all kindes, as conveyances and deliverers of me to you, whether you accept me as a friend, or as a patient, or as a penitent, or as a beadsman, for I decline no jurisdiction, or refuse any tenure. I would not open any doore upon you, but look in when you open it. Angels have not, nor affect not other knowledge of one another, then they list to reveal to one another. It is then in this onely, that friends are Angels, that they are capable and fit for such revelations when they are offered.[28]

In 'Negative Love' Donne says he has never 'stoop'd so low' as those who love the body, and:

> Seldome to them, which soare no higher
> Then vertue or the minde to admire.

He does not know what he loves, though he knows what he does not. Similarly in the letter to Goodyer he resorts to negatives, disowning various motives for writing letters as 'either above or under' his own motive; and his own motive is ultimately not to have a motive: 'I would not open any doore upon you, but look in when you open it.'

The last two sentences, which introduce the comparison with angelic modes of knowledge, are complicated, and at first the comparison seems to work the wrong way round. If Donne is sending unspecific, all-purpose letters to Goodyer, so that Goodyer (like Bridget White) can choose what meaning or motive to ascribe to them, then the freedom of choice

[28] *Letters*, pp. 109–12.

would seem to belong to the observer, Goodyer, who selects what traits he wishes to observe in his friend Donne, or in his letters. But that is actually the opposite of the practice among angels, as Donne describes it. For with angels the freedom of choice belongs to the observed, who reveals to observers only such knowledge about himself as he cares to reveal. The angelic comparison can be made to work only if we realize that Donne is the supposed observer. He imagines that his letters have transported him physically into Goodyer's presence: they are quite literally 'conveyances and deliverers of me to you'. Being in Goodyer's presence, he can observe him, but (and this is the point of the letters' lack of specificity) he does not envisage observing him in any self-assertive or buttonholing way. He will see only what Goodyer wishes to be seen, as angels do: 'I would not open any doore upon you, but looke in when you open it.' It is as if the bundle of Donne's letters in Goodyer's room were conscious, but used its consciousness tactfully and discreetly, noticing only such facets of Goodyer as he chooses to expose, and saying only what he wants to hear.

The extraordinary thing about the passage, of course, is that though it is really Goodyer who is engaged in observing, since he is using his eyes to read Donne's letters, Donne has imaginatively animated his letters so completely that he writes as if he, or they, were scrutinizing Goodyer, while Goodyer reads, and waiting for an opportunity to come up with just the meaning that Goodyer would choose himself. It is, for Donne's period, a distinctly sophisticated account of the reading process. Instead of the reader reading the written page, the written page reads the reader, looking in through whatever 'doore' into his mind the reader chooses to open, and eliciting so much of his character as, in his interpretation of the written page, he reveals.

Fancying that his letters carried him bodily into another's presence was one way, for Donne, of surmounting distance and solitude, as in his valedictions and other poems he repeatedly struggles to do. He seems to have felt the insuf-

ficiency of his aloneness ('No man is an island') as much as he
felt his distinctness and singularity ('Nothing else is'). Letters
satisified both his egotism and his wish for company, for they
allowed him to transpose his personality into an alien space
and time, as well as to achieve communion with another soul.
The claim that he and his letters are physically interchangeable
is made first and most vehemently in a verse-letter to Rowland
Woodward of August 1597:[29]

> Seeme, when thou read'st these lines, to dreame of me,
> Never did Morpheus nor his brother weare
> Shapes soe like those shapes, whom they would appeare,
> As this my letter is like me, for it
> Hath my name, words, hand, feet, heart, minde and wit;
> It is my deed of gift of mee to thee,
> It is my Will, my selfe the Legacie.
> So thy retyrings I love, yea envie,
> Bred in thee by a wise melancholy,
> That I rejoyce, that unto where thou art,
> Though I stay here, I can thus send my heart.

So intensely personal a notion of what a letter entails (a dream
of the sender, sent by post) naturally deters the inclusion of
non-personal items, and it is no surprise for us, by now, to find
Donne telling Woodward in the following lines that he has
nothing of general interest to report ('All newes I thinke
sooner reach thee then mee').

In his 'Negative Love' letter to Goodyer Donne imagines
his various and intermittent letters accumulating so as to
become a second self in Goodyer's keeping. The notion of
himself being dispersed, randomly scattered abroad, and then
safely collected, appealed strongly to his imagination, and he
eventually found the most satisfying correlative to it in the
Christian doctrine of the resurrection of the body, which is a
favourite topic in the sermons. But the idea of a body of letters
acquiring life in Goodyer's presence affords an alternative

[29] *Satires* etc., ed. Milgate. p. 64.

matrix for this imagined process, and when Donne writes to Goodyer from France about a disruption of postal deliveries which is causing early letters to arrive after later ones, the resurrection of the body and the collection of its scattered dust seems to be at the back of his mind:

> But Sir, if our Letters come not in due order, and so make not a certain and concurrent chain, yet if they come as Atomes, and so meet at last, by any crooked and casuall application, they make up, and they nourish bodies of friendship.[30]

'Atomes' meeting to make up 'bodies' inevitably recall, for the reader of Donne's sermons, such outbursts as that in the Bridgewater marriage sermon of 1627:

> Where be all the Atoms of that flesh, which a *Corrasive* hath eat away, or a *Consumption* hath breath'd, and exhal'd away from our arms, and other limbs? . . . God . . . beckens for the bodies of his Saints, and in the twinckling of an eye, that body that was scattered over all the elements, is sate down at the right hand of God, in a glorious resurrection.[31]

On the last day the divine sorting office will ensure, as Donne never tires of explaining, that one's scattered particles will be dissociated from those of all the other dead. Donne dwells on this because it accords with his deep concern for personal exclusiveness. That his body could, even after it had been reduced to dust, be identified and isolated, was an ego-endorsing belief and mattered to him for the same reason as it mattered to him to dismiss the busy concerns of the alien world ('Goe tell Court-huntsmen, that the King will ride'). The exclusion of outside concerns from his letters belongs to the same complex.

The existence of Donne's newsless letters is not, then, as

[30] *Letters*, pp. 73–4.
[31] John Donne, *Sermons*, ed. G.R. Potter and E.M. Simpson, Berkeley and Los Angeles, 1953–62, viii, 98.

puzzling as commentators have found it to be. Given his imaginative predispositions, it is exactly what we should expect. Such letters reflect his jealous sense of identity, as well as his interest in soul transference and the integrity of love and friendship. Being unlike any previous models they illustrate too, as do his poems, his inclination to evolve new literary modes to meet the special demands of his personality. How, when you write to a friend or lover, do you keep out the interfering, impersonal world? If you do keep it out, what do you write about? Do you exist at all, in isolation? Or does identity define itself only in reaction to externals? These were the problems Donne faced. His letters, which transmit only the self-involved windings of his own consciousness, are the answer.

IV

Herbert's Ground

M.C. BRADBROOK

God is the ground of our being, and therefore cannot be the object of our thought.

THIS aphorism—which I think must be Tillich's, which Henry Chadwick would amend to 'adequate thought'— might recall to those who find Herbert a poet to live with, that all his varied patterns work on them, to borrow a metaphor from T.S. Eliot, like the piece of meat the burglar throws to the watchdog. Poet and reader alike are laid open to permeative and pervasive intimations, that reach beyond consciousness and in the words of Dryden 'move the sleeping images of things towards the light', things hard for thought, *forti cose a pensar*, for which Dante invoked the Muses—powers that are above the conscious mind.[1]

The emblematic precision of Herbert's images should not disguise their generalized appeal to taste, smell, muscular and vasodilatory registers. Differing alike from the wit of Donne and the eroticism of Crashaw, depending on obscurer and more animal responses, they were early set to strong musical rhythms, by Herbert himself and by others. Today the penumbra brought out by the setting of 'The Elixir' or 'Praise II'—for instance a descant in the last verse of 'The Elixir'—reinforces what Eliot terms the 'magic' of

---

[1] 'Things hard to be understood' (2 Peter, 1:16) is quoted by Herbert on Valdesso (*Works*, ed. Hutchinson, p. 317), but I am indebted for the parallel with *Purgatorio* XXIX, 42, and the quotation from Dryden to L.C. Knights (*International Review of Psychoanalysis*, 7, 125–36). In the preface to *The Temple*, Ferrar claims a higher inspiration than the Muses as Herbert's 'confident' assertion.

Church-bels beyond the starres heard, the souls bloud,
The land of spices, something understood
('Prayer I', 13–14)

The regular and insistent call to public worship which Herbert
obeyed twice daily throughout his life is also felt like a pulse in
the body, reason is joined to spicy odour and taste in the four
noun clauses that conclude this English sonnet.[2]

If 'genius is essentially the capacity to deal effectually with
impulses at the state of formation when they are still only
roughly affective states'[3] very extensive ordering may precede
intellectual formulation or even general awareness. The pre-
conscious resolution of a conflict may precede its recognition
(and verbalization). This may help to account for Herbert's
being 'understood' in such diverse ways by believers and
unbelievers.

It is a commonplace that Herbert's emotional roots were
familial; of his six brothers, three were poets, one of no mean
achievement, one a Master of the Revels at court. The three
sisters were bookish. Three other brothers were soldiers or
sailors—and the eldest of the family, Lord Herbert of Cherbury, recorded that George 'was not exempt from passion and
choler, being infirmities to which all our race is subject'. Their
mother, Magdalen Herbert, widowed when George was
three, raised this family of ten and kept them together so that
Lord Herbert could write to Henry sadly in 1643: 'And here I
must remember that of us all, there remains but you and I to
brother it'. Donne described them as 'a family united to God
and within itself'.

Henry, from 1623 Master of the Revels at the Court, and

---

[2] Compare the different effect of Donne's 'Her pure, and eloquent
blood/Spoke in her cheeks and so distinctly wrought/That one might almost
say, her body thought'.

[3] See D.W. Harding, *Experience into Words*, 1963, p. 183, quoting Thur-
stone. He adds 'In some minds the language processes reflect not only the
main experience . . . but also much subtler features of the preverbal experience and features of which the writer himself may have no awareness except
through the overtones of what he finds himself writing' (p. 187).

next below George in age, resembled him as a portrait of *L'Allegro* might resemble one of *Il Penseroso*—the features are very similar, but D'Artagnan's moustaches bristle above the courtier's fine lace. Henry knew worldly success; promoted to office by his kinsman, the Earl of Pembroke, Lord Chamberlain, within twelve months he had secured a rich City widow and two estates. *The Church Porch* was probably written for Henry about 1615[4] on his visit to France. All were accomplished linguists; Lord Herbert an Ambassador to France, Henry serving a French Queen (and making his notes in French), George collecting his 'Outlandish' proverbs from the modern languages. All wrote in Latin; George's professional career at Cambridge was in languages. He was fellow of Trinity for twelve years, Public Orator in the University for eight, and gave his Rede Lectures in rhetoric. Both George and Henry were roused by indecorous language; Walton records that George displayed too much zeal in correcting indecencies of behaviour in church or gabbled prayer, and Henry was even stricter than his master, Charles I, in expunging oaths from the plays he censored. George stayed with Henry a good deal (and may for instance have seen the last of Jonson's Jacobean masques, *The Fortunate Isles*);[5] as soon as he had a house of his own, he imported three orphan nieces.

The deepest natural impress on him was therefore that of a large family, balanced and distributed attachments; and secondly the habits of the University. The George Herbert who translated for the Chancellor of Cambridge, Francis Bacon, his *Advancement of Learning*, and who was consulted by Lord Herbert on the orthodoxy of *De Veritate*, which in private was dedicated to him, should scarcely have been censured for 'a constitutional inability to sustain speculation' even if 'he could

---

[4] See Amy M. Charles, *A Life of George Herbert*, 1977, p. 78.
[5] Sir Henry supervised costume, as we learn from his Record Book (which survives only in extracts) and presumably arranged the royal rehearsals.

not resolve speculative poems with speculative resolutions'.[6] He was engaged in a rhetorical enterprise; his poems were to be published if, and only if, they were likely 'to turn to the advantage of any dejected poor soul'; Walton's hagiography is now supported by the Ferrar papers on this point. The title page of the beautifully printed 12mo that issued from the sign of the Angel on Market Hill described Herbert as 'late Orator of the University of Cambridge', not Rector of Bemerton. The printer, Thomas Buck, Herbert's contemporary, and Fellow of St Catharine's, had standards unrivalled in the country, and for Herbert he did his best, so that the first five editions of *The Temple* actually improve the text instead of corrupting it, with small emendations from Herbert's lost original. More dentelles and a border of a Church Porch were added.

The Press had published the Orator's Latin verses from 1620 onwards (he was then twenty-seven); these bring him far closer to Edward and Henry than do his English poems. Sharp-witted, hyperbolical, rather contemptuously dismissive of dissent and extreme Calvinism, they reveal a shadow self or anti-self of the other Herbert. The most famous was his address to Bacon, in praise of *Instauratio Magna*, written very shortly before the Chancellor's disgrace in 1621. Habits of public orators do not change; it is not unlike Dr Stubbings's tropes today in praise of science:

> signa . . . non dubitanda . . .
> quorum ope germanus, vultis quocumque vagari
> undique cognosci QUARX sine fraude potest.

Bacon is Archpriest of Truth; Lord of St Albans and of the Inductive Method; Literary Brutus, casting off the Yoke of

[6] Herbert of Cherbury says in his *Autobiography* that Grotius and Tilenus also read *De Veritate*, published in Paris 1624. B.L. Sloane MS 3597, dated 15 December 1622, carries the dedication to George. See Amy Charles, p. 89. The two quotations are from Helen Vendler, *The Poetry of George Herbert*, 1975, pp. 193, 195; her chapter 2, 'The re-invented poem' is representative of the attitude she shares with Stanley Fish (*Self-Consuming Artefacts*, 1972), and sets the approach for modern critics.

Books; Atlas of Nature; the *tour de force* has its absurdities, such as Gimlet of Sincerity, and its subtleties such as Priest both of the World and of its Soul—building up to the final collapse: '*O me probè lassum! Iuuate, Posteri!*'

In the light of Herbert's strong words to Bacon about the state of the University Library, and his plea to his family that he might pledge his annuity to buy books, for which he was already forgoing his dinner, the epigram to King James, who had presented his *Opera Latina*, must not be read as outrageous flattery so much as well turned mendicancy:

> *Quid Vaticanam Bodleiúmque obijcis, Hospes?*
> *Vnicus est nobis Bibliotheca Liber.*

He gave his Rede Lectures on the rhetoric of King James, who thought him the University's 'jewel'. The rhetorical as distinct from the committed self[7] wrote the verses for Prince Henry and the recently discovered lines addressed to the Elector Palatine; the public orator, rather than the son, within a week or so of her death, wrote the Greek and Latin elegy for Lady Danvers; it was appended to Donne's sermon at her 'month's mind'. The most filial part is VII, where he says he is really very ill, won't she come back and talk to him? On the whole, Herbert wrote to mortals in Latin verse; the lost dispute with Bishop Andrewes on predestination and sanctity of life (Andrewes always carried Herbert's letter next his heart) was in Greek.

Among the personal poems in English, the verses for Princess Elizabeth, Queen of Bohemia, recently discovered in a Cambridge MS in an early version, are datable 1622.[8] This poem of consolation was written for her refuge at the Hague.

---

[7] For this distinction see Richard A. Lanham, *The Motives of Eloquence*, 1976, ch. 1.

[8] Cambridge MS Add. 4138. See *Transactions of the Cambridge Bibliographical Society* VII (2), 1978, 156–69; for a text see T–L. Petworth, *English Literary Renaissance*, Winter 1979, pp. 108–20; for that to the Elector Palatine, see L. Bradner, 'New Poems by George Herbert', *Renaissance News* 15 (1962), pp. 208–11.

Three of Herbert's brothers had fought for the Protestant cause in the Netherlands, and two had died there—William in 1617, Richard this same year. The Earl of Pembroke had briefly commanded a company in 1620. In the watery realm of the Netherlands, Elizabeth's tears serve to foster the fruitful growth that will be sent to recover her fortunes—her off-spring.

> Shine on, majestic soul, abide
> Like David's tree, planted beside
> The Flemish rivers . . .
>
> (68–9)

The poem resembles both the consolations and the satires of that later master of Latin and English verse, Andrew Marvell. The paradox of fruitful mourning offers hope in a desperate situation, for the English expeditionary force under Sir Horace Vere was besieged and starving. Herbert has too bitter a knowledge of war to counsel it, but Hell waits, for the only time in Herbert, in this political context. Hell is for Hapsburgs.

The plea for peace which Herbert as public orator delivered to Charles Prince of Wales and the Duke of Buckingham on their visit to Cambridge in October 1623 would have been agreed with the Heads of Houses, for Herbert knew it was no function of the Orator to speak his own sentiments; but as he also well knew, it would blast his prospects. War with Spain, in revenge for the refusal of the proposed Spanish marriage for which they had gone to Madrid was now being urged on all sides, not least by the Earl of Pembroke. Nevertheless, Sir Henry Herbert's masque for Twelfth Night, written by Ben Jonson, had to be postponed and revised because of its anti-Spanish sentiments and in the following April Lord Herbert was recalled in disgrace from his embassy in Paris; his out-spoken and far-sighted advice had clearly proved an embar-rassment. Any hopes that George might have entertained of the diplomatic career on which the Orator's office had launched his predecessors, Naunton and Nethersole, were lost.

In 1624, also, the government completed the destruction of the Virginia Company in which his stepfather Sir John Danvers had an interest, and of which Nicholas Ferrar was Treasurer. This year George briefly sat in Parliament for the family seat (the master of his college was facing a charge there; he was John Richardson, Regius Professor of Divinity and reputed an Arminian). In November 1624, as his fellowship required, Herbert took Deacon's orders; next year Nicholas Ferrar retired to Little Gidding to found his 'Arminian nunnery' whilst Lord Herbert retreated to Montgomery Castle and his library. The inscription on his tomb was to record of all his achievements only that he was *auctor libri, qui titulus est de Veritate*.

For Lord Herbert the Defence of Truth was the defence of religion—there was no other word than God for what later philosophers were to term 'the whole thing'. Although Ben Jonson praised him for piety, and although *De Veritate*, published in Paris in 1624, was to be licensed by Laud, Edward was later contrasted with the author of *The Temple* for his neglect of the Incarnation. They come closest in Lord Herbert's notion of 'plastic virtue' or 'harmony of the soul' which, in anticipation of the Cambridge Platonists, animates his universe:

> Anyone who refuses to look for the law by which these principles combine with our own in the mind or harmony of the world, that plastic power which reduces different kinds of food to one form, may learn to know it through his inner consciousness.
>
> (*De Veritate*, tr. Carré, 1937, p. 169)[9]

This harmony of the world is presented by George Herbert as Platonic in the last and best section of *Passio Discerpta*, written the same year as *De Veritate*:

[9] For this passage I am indebted to R.D. Bedford, *The Defence of Truth; Herbert of Cherbury and the Seventeenth Century*, 1979, pp. 105–6. He points out also that the *Autobiography* was a private family document, and the partially jesting, self-mocking effect must correct the common reading as naive bragging.

Non moreris solus: Mundus simul interit in te,
Agnoscitque tuam Machina tota Crucem.
Hunc ponas animan mundi, Plato; vel tua mundum
Ne nimium vexet quaestio, pone meam.

You do not die alone; the world at the same time dies with
You, the whole machine is one with Your cross. Plato, in
Him find the harmony of the world—or if your search
vexes the world, see Him in me.

       (In Mundi sympathiam cum Christo)

The Passion and Crucifixion were to be throughout Herbert's
poetry the dominant theme in his treatment of the Incarnation.
Mourning and fruitfulness are here, in a different dimension.

 The Temple is entirely about personal relationships,
although other human beings than Jesus are not the subject of
it. It is intimate without being personal. Hence its strong
maieutic power for readers. It is also sensuous without being
erotic. This cannot be said of his Latin poems.

 In 'Man', Herbert found all symmetry,

> Full of proportions, one limb to another,
> And all to all the world besides:
> Each part may call the farthest, brother:
> For head with foot hath private amitie,
> And both with moons and tides.

             (14–18)

The world unites in man's service; the different parts of Scriptures are organically linked ('The H. Scriptures II'), whilst in
'Providence', as the consciousness of Nature, Man is ordained
priest to render thanks for the extraordinary cohesion of the
whole thing. This is rehearsed in a lengthy piece of natural
history ranging from coconuts to crocodiles.

 Though Bacon did not accept the theory of *spiritus mundi*,
which he attributed to the Pythagoreans (*Sylva Sylvarum*,
Century X, 900), yet in his little book of the translation of the

psalms, Nature's praise, in Psalm 104—the only one in which his painful lines take fire—indicates the model for Herbert in 'Providence'. In Bacon, the glory of the birds, and the ocean where 'the greater navies look like walking woods' and Leviathan 'makes the seas to seeth like boiling pan' balance the laments of Psalm 90; in his disgrace and sickness, he also used Psalms 1 and 137, which Herbert had applied to the Queen of Bohemia. Bacon's little volume is dedicated to his 'friend', the Orator, as thanks for what Herbert had done for him.

> It being my manner for dedications, to choose those that I hold most fit for the argument, I thought that in respect of divinity and poetry met, whereof the one is the matter, the other the style of this little writing, I could not make better choice.

This was 1625; within a year Bacon died and one of Herbert's last acts as Public Orator, though no official duty, was to make up a volume of verse tributes to Bacon's memory.

The use of the Psalms in English, a main strand in the constant daily exercise of worship which was implanted from infancy in Herbert, provided a powerful integrative force for his imagination. It has often been observed that they pervade his English poetry to an extent unmatched by any other English poet. The great metrical variety of the version composed by Sir Philip Sidney and the Countess of Pembroke at Wilton, within a few miles of Bemerton Rectory, offered an example within the family. By 1640, there were over three hundred versions of the Psalms in English; they had been among the first parts of Scripture to be translated, e.g. by Richard Rolle; and the psalm as ground and pattern of poetic sequences has been traced both in Shakespeare and Milton (who translated some at the age of fifteen).[10]

In his funeral sermon for Herbert's mother, Donne recalled that she was in the habit of 'shutting up' each Sunday's private prayers at home 'with a psalm'. At Westminster School,

George would have attended the Abbey services, where Coverdale's version was used; at Cambridge, as well as daily attendance in his college chapel, he would have been bound to attend Great St Mary's as public orator. As deacon, he would be required to recite morning and evening prayer daily; when instituted in 1626 into the Canonry of Leighton Ecclesia he would be expected to recite daily the two psalms assigned to the holder of that office, 31 and 32; over his stall is carved '*In te, Domine, speravi*' from Psalm 31. At Little Gidding the entire Psalter was recited in the chapel every twenty-four hours. The psalms were equally in use amongst all shades of Anglicans and dissenters. The poetic books of the Bible were often issued separately.

In the psalms, complaint and lament alternate with consolation in a personal voice, for they are at once individual and representative of the people of Israel. Violent and often primitive emotions are combined with musical order; personal dereliction is given a corporate form, supplying a sense of integration and solidarity which brings to the surface 'things hard for thought'. The powerful monotheism is set in a pastoral world, and this in turn is reinterpreted in the light of the life of Jesus, who himself made use of Psalms—the Cry from the Cross that comes from Psalm 22, again in turn, brings in images of the Holy Communion. There the ingestion of substance is part of a ritual of grace that relies on the lowliest of the senses—taste and smell—on kinaesthetic imagery in Herbert of growth and the diurnal rhythms that accompany life even in sleep:

[10] For the general influence of the Psalms, see Barbara K. Lewalski, *Protestant Poetics and the Seventeenth Century Religious Lyric*, 1979, ch. 9. Miss Lewalski takes issue with Helen Vendler's method (p. 301). For the effect of the Psalms on Herbert see *The English Poems of George Herbert*, ed. C.A. Patrides, 1974, pp. 9–10 and notes *passim*; I am also indebted to a privately printed pamphlet by Margaret Bottrall. For Sidney's influence, see Louis Martz, *The Poetry of Meditation*, 1954, p. 273. For the influence of the Psalms on Shakespeare, see Kenneth Muir, *Shakespeare's Sonnets*, 1979, pp. 10–13; for Milton, see M.A. Radzinowicz, *Toward 'Samson Agonistes'*, 1978. ch. 10.

> But by the way of nourishment and strength
> Thou creep'st into my breast;
> Making thy way my rest,
> And thy small quantities my length;
> Which spread their forces into every part.
>   ('The H. Communion', 7–11)

Such poems as 'The Invitation' and 'The Banquet' (where the bread smells freshly and sugar melts in wine) relate the sacred elements (pomanders that have been bruised are sweetest) to the august event transforming all relations between God and the world. Its sublimation lies in 'Love III'.

Herbert himself versified directly the best known of the Psalms, the one taught to children, Psalm 23, where he incorporates a phrase from Sternhold and Hopkins, the popular version used by the humblest. On the other hand his characteristic rhythm of one long line followed by an answering short line which serve for question and reply, represents the Hebraic parallelism. 'Antiphon II' depends on the chapel seating of men and boys in a choir, when psalms are sung in answering verses; as for instance at the opening of Psalm 76: 'In Jewry is God known: his name is great in Israel'. The echoes in a harmonious universe, like the sympathies between parts of the body or parts of the scriptures are reflected in the harmonious unity of the Body of Christ at the end ('Dooms-day', 29–30) and those 'Church-bels beyond the starres heard' in 'Heaven' (a poem which parodies one by Lord Herbert, 'Echo to the Rock'). If the Herbert brothers exchanged poems, they would constitute George Herbert's first audience; the family at Little Gidding had regular sessions for story-telling, the stories being written out later. Circulation in the family was Sir Philip Sidney's practice—it happened later in Jane Austen's and in many Victorian families. If *The Church Porch* were written for Sir Henry, it is probable that the rather poor verses on St Mary Magdalen were a name-day poem for Herbert's mother (Donne wrote her one also). 'The Quiddity' could have been provoked by Edward. The first third of *The*

Temple which survives in the Williams MS, if dated
1613–1618, belongs to the early Cambridge years, and the
afflictions there include the deaths of two brothers (William
the soldier, and Charles, the brilliant young poet and Fellow of
New College, Oxford, one year older than George), the
beginning of his sister Elizabeth's long sickness, and a very
serious illness of his own. Amy Charles dates 'Affliction I'
from this period.[11] 'The Quip' paradoxically unites the
memories of those little quarrelsome dialogues given as plays
at Trinity College (such as *Band, Cuff and Ruff*, 1615, or *Sword,
Rapier and Dagger*, also 1615) and the anguish of Psalm 38,
which provides the refrain. Perhaps as a young Fellow Herbert
shared in *The Battle of Affections or Love's Loadstone*, the Trinity
College play for this year; they were usually given in the Lent
Term.

In distinction to Lord Herbert, George Herbert sees Truth
in two aspects, the 'two rare cabinets full of treasure' being
'The Trinity and the Incarnation', both of which have been
unlocked, yet 'the statelier cabinet, the Trinity' by its 'sparkling light access denies' in this life. We are allured with delights
to the Incarnation:

> Because this box we know;
> For we have all of us just such another.
>
> ('Ungratefulness', 23–4)

Herbert's concentration on the Passion story, in both Latin
and English poems, begins with the utmost perversity of man,
in using against the Creator the Creator's own powers—'They
use that power against me, which I gave' ('The Sacrifice' l.
11)—the obverse of which is found in 'The Dedication' where
the first fruits of poetry are returned, remembering that *'from
thee they came'*. This is also the theme of the final dedication in

---

[11] Amy M. Charles, pp. 84–7. She thinks the lack of 'employment' was
met by the election as Public Orator in 1620; Herbert refers to this elsewhere
as his employment.

Musae Responsoriae which is addressed '*Ad Deum*' but concerns the Third Person:

> *O dulcissime Spiritus,*
> *Sanctos qui gemitus mentibus inseris*
> *A Te Turture defluos,*
> *Quòd scribo, & placeo, si placeo, tuum est.*

O most sweet Spirit, who permeates with holy sorrow, that flows from you, my Dove; whatever I write, the gratification of others, if they are gratified, comes from you.

This paradox—used for the words of the Offertory in the present Communion service—obliterates the sense of mine and thine, till in the words of Shakespeare's 'The Phoenix and the Turtle', 'either was the other's mine'. The theme of 'Affliction III' is 'what is happening in me is happening in you' and Christ makes it 'A point of honour, now to grieve in me' (15); in 'Unkindness', the sinners 'Let the poore/And thou within them, starve at doore' (13–14). Herbert's version of 'The Phoenix and The Turtle' is 'The Holdfast' and 'Clasping of hands', both titles symbolizing a marriage. As the expropriation of the self proceeds, there is a kind of playfulness in the love-competition of 'Artillerie' where 'I am thine;/I must be so, if I am mine'; and in 'Justice I' the argument runs 'I think you are behaving badly to me; then I see I am behaving in exactly the same way to you!' In 'Conscience', which opens the later group of poems, an attitude of mature tolerance towards inner feelings of guilt is made possible through the power of the Holy Communion. In 'Gratefulnesse' the skilful mendicant gives away his case to God, as he never did to King James:

> Thou that hast giv'n so much to me,
> Give one thing more, a grateful heart.
> See how thy beggar works on thee
> By art.

(1–4)

'The Thanksgiving' and 'The Reprisal', both early poems, show the pressure of pain in the impossibility of any recompense; but this pain is left behind, and the anthropomorphic consolations also disappear. The deeper sense of dereliction and desolation marks spiritual advance but cannot be discerned whilst it is in progress; this is the common pattern of the inner life. 'Deniall', 'Affliction IV' and 'Grief' may rank with Hopkins' 'terrible sonnets'; Hopkins once observed, 'the greater the consciousness, the greater the pain'. About a third of the poems in *The Temple* are variations on spiritual pain.

The Temple is full of contradictory moods, sometimes emphasized by contradictory titles. Herbert felt obliged to withhold canonization from saints and angels since he found no scriptural warrant, yet he wrote one English and several Latin poems to saints. 'The British Church' praises his 'dear mother' for her comeliness, half way between Rome and Geneva; in 'Church-rents and Schismes', by an anticipation of Blake, she is a 'sick rose'. Poetry should be plain ('Jordan I') yet artful ('Praise II'). His attachments were to all parties; during his early Cambridge years 1609–1615 Lancelot Andrewes, known in boyhood, was at Ely; later they disputed on predestination and sanctity of life together; yet later, Ferrar and Bishop Williams, both his friends, were at opposite poles doctrinally. Herbert's predestinarian view was, as for most in his time, a joyful doctrine, as his very cheerful 'Doomsday' and 'Judgment' celebrate. He thinks that even Pharoah and Judas, vessels of wrath as they are, need 'discreet, and wary explaining' as to reprobation (*Notes on Valdesso*, No. 49). Perhaps like Perkins, the Puritan Elizabethan (who died in 1601), he moved from an earlier strictness when he became a pastor. In 'Judgment', his own sins are simply handed back to God the Judge with the words 'They are thine'—purchased at the cost described in 'The Agony'. Herbert on the Atonement often uses financial images; but he also wrote a sharply satiric poem beginning 'Money . . .' In 'Obedience', he invites the reader to deed himself to God in exchange for His gift. Like others in the family, Herbert suffered from melancholy; the fighting inner selves of 'The Quip' and 'The Family' alternate with the more terrible flat despaire of 'Deniall', and the modulation is given in 'The Flower':

> And now in age I bud again,
> After so many deaths, I live and write:
> I once more smell the dew and rain . . .
>
> (36–8)

—more lightly in 'Giddiness'. His remedy for those 'in the military state' is given in *The Country Parson* (XXXIV). To those near despair he offers this 'unanswerable' argument: if God hates them, it is either as Creatures or as sinful. But the perfect Artist *must* love what he has created; and he who gave himself in the Incarnation *must* love them much more. This is double ratification, and the faultier the sinner, the greater God's love.

> And all may certainly conclude, that God loves them, till either they despise that love, or despair of his mercy; not any sin else but is within his love; but the despising of his love must needs be without it. The thrusting away of his arm makes us only not embraced.

When Herbert finally committed himself to the priesthood, he never spoke of Jesus without adding 'My Master', which Ferrar in the preface to *The Temple* said was to testify 'of his independency of all others'. 'The Odour' describes these most uncompromising words as 'spicinesse' and 'a broth of smells'. In contemporary England the powers of a master were legal and specific; one of Shakespeare's most unpleasant characters refuses to apply the word to anyone but God (*All's Well that Ends Well*, II,iii,238–44). Herbert himself in *The Country Parson* (X) distinguishes between the servants and the children, both are kept between love and fear, 'but to children he shews more love than terror, to his servants more terror than love; but an old good servant boards a child.'

The term indicates the subjection of his will. The kinaes-

thetic images of 'The Pulley' and 'The Collar', explicit only in
the titles, can be felt in the alternating long and short lines—
which work like the 'moles' that 'Heave and cast about' in
'Confession'. 'The Pulley' is Augustinian—'Thou hast made
us for thyself; and our hearts can find no rest until they rest in
thee'. These are both late poems. 'The Collar' is a revolt from
the Communion ('I struck the board and cry'd—No more')
and the response is not to a servant but to a child. The Grace is
irresistible. It also could be painful.

The lyrics are described as 'private ejaculations'; they are not
doctrinal. Poetry was for Herbert the most inclusive form of
experience ('The Quiddity'), a practice of the presence of God.
Modern criticism delights to rewrite Herbert, and also to
stress the idea that he himself 'rewrote' his poems (the title of a
chapter in Helen Vendler's book). A recent work, *Overheard by
God* (1980), compounds the approach of Mrs Vendler, and of
Stanley Fish, with the formalism of Kermode; it is by *The
Genesis of Secresy* out of *Self-Consuming Artefacts*, erudite and
fashionable.

In this book, A.D. Nuttall appreciates the agony of Herbert's conflicts but adds some of his own, presented largely in
philosophic puzzles (one of his previous books dealt with
solipsism). After a few needlings about Herbert's 'bad faith'
(p. 9) and 'bumptiousness' (p. 15), Nuttall uses Herbert to
conduct a quarrel with Calvin's God, the God of double
predestination, of supralapsarianism, of 'that awesome decree'
which Calvin thought he found in scripture. Faced with the
doctrine of total depravity (p. 79), deprived of the Holy Spirit
('It would appear that we have only one friend in the Trinity',
p. 23), Herbert is saved unconsciously, and never knows he is
saved, from Calvin's God:

> What Herbert's poetry does is to fasten on those aspects of
> the moral life which are *essentially* creaturely, which simply
> make no sense if transferred to the Creator, namely surren-
> der, trust, faith, submission, love. To give these to God is
> not to reform ethics but to destroy it. (p. 79)

The author of 'The Agonie' is thus deprived of the Jesus of Gethsemane. The different aspects of the one God shewn in the Trinity is a scandal to some, and foolishness to others. That the author of 'The British Church' and 'Church-rents and Schismes', not to mention *Musae Responsoriae*, had reservations about Genevan doctrine cannot be questioned; in 'The Watercourse', God decides on Salvation and Damnation for man; but tears offer true cleansing. However, Nuttall selects his emphasis:

> It was not I but the author of *Jordan* I and II who affirmed that only the plainest truth would do for devotion. It was not I but a theology still potent in Herbert's time that affirmed that every effort to deserve the love of God was a kind of pride. (p. 140)

Nuttall enjoys thinking that no Anglican would read Herbert as he does (p. 51, p. 69). He might have added the Free Churchmen, I would think, especially Eglwys Methodistiaid Calfinaidd; for one of Herbert's selves was a hymn-singing Welshman.

Empson spent much energy killing Milton's God, but Nuttall gets Herbert to do it for him—though of course if his 'Herbert' realized what he had said he 'would fight like a tiger' against the words (p. 80). There is certainly a tiger about somewhere, for Calvin's God is killed more than once (see also p. 75).

Herbert cut out from *The Temple* the early 'Perseverence', presumably as unlikely to bring comfort to poor dejected souls. It rather powerfully shows the speaker as a baby at the breast and God as mother.

The 'bad faith' of prideful humility is related by Nuttall to the puzzle of the pronouns. How can Herbert put words in God's mouth, and offer them to God as coming from Him? 'The Dedication' and 'The Holdfast' are worried vigorously. The deepest dilemma for any priest is how to enact the very person of Christ, as administrator at the Holy Communion, and also receive it. To dress up as God, and watch how well you are doing it, as Herbert's care for comeliness would require, is the theme of 'Aaron'. Verbalization pales beside this—but Nuttall is concerned only with dogmatics, not *doing* theology (though he seems too to think all the poems were written after Herbert was priested). The complexity and cross-strands of doctrine during Herbert's forty years means the whole web must be seen; but on p. 53 Nuttall disposes of all the parts of divinity he considers irrelevant to Calvin's God. Moving on to Milton and Dante, he ends with the 'fiction' of the Fourth Gospel. Finally he comes to the Man behind the fictions, and offers, as a solution to the divine claim, the suggestion, which he appears to think original, that Jesus was 'mad' (p. 142). It is hardly a clinical term, but the view was temporally held by some of great authority (Mark, 3).

More than half this book is devoted to killing 'Calvin's God', who is termed 'Herbert's God'—as some people put into the mouths of their pet dogs the things they would like to say themselves.[12] Nuttall's Herbert is none the less worth

[12] From Calvin and the XXXIX Articles, Nuttall extracts the view that 'God the Father really hates us' (p. 23). General Calvinism swung from the high position of the 1580s and Perkins, to the point where Walton wrote Herbert's *Life* to attack it. Herbert's Church was, and is, truly ecumenical. Whilst conceding that Herbert need not have been as radical as he assumes, Nuttall (p. 53), dropping the *Book of Common Prayer*, the Spirit and the Sacrament, creates his problems, stages confrontations, with 'fine nets and stratagems to catch us in', 'millions of surprises'. His emotion is betrayed in the jocularity with which he invents roles for the defeated God (pp. 51–2), dramatizes the 'downcast eyes and modest smile' with which Calvin accepts that '*The Institutes* was not written by Calvin; it was written by God' (p. 25), or in plain bumptiousness injects an irrelevance where Eliot found incantation:

Prayer is defined (sic) by Herbert as 'God's breath in man returning to his birth' (*Prayer 1*). The image is very beautiful but at the same time obscurely troubling. Most of us prefer fresh air to CO_2. (p. 33)

He also does his best (p. 260) to neutralize passages, like that I have quoted from *The Country Parson* (XXXIV), which are explicit about the love of God for sinners.

It seems to me that belief in predestination implies no more cohesion than does membership of the Labour Party today. These had been the doctrines of

putting with the others, as evidence of Herbert's maieutic powers; he is among the most 'open' of poets. He was read simultaneously by the imprisoned Charles I and by the New Englanders; he was rewritten by Wesley; and that unbeliever, E. M. Forster, carried a little red-bound fine copy on journeys.

According to Nuttall, Herbert had a death-wish (p. 62). At all events, he had a very bad illness in 1610, 1615, and 1623, and eventually developed tuberculosis. As several of the family died young, it is probable that Herbert was soon intuitively aware of his fatal condition. 'The Crosse' records his anguish in religious terms, 'Home' and 'The Forerunners' in more human fashion (Teilhard de Chardin, in *Le Milieu Divin*, meets 'the diminishings' sacramentally). Herbert entertains none of the illusions of *spes phthisica*, but recalls his prebendal psalm, 31. Like Keats's, his natural sensibilities seem to have been heightened, and as in his early poem to Elizabeth of Bohemia, death is associated with the alternate principle of growth; in a late poem, the flowers,

> . . . so sweetly deaths sad taste convey,
> Making my minde to smell my fatall day;
> Yet sugring the suspicion

that

> I follow straight without complaints or grief,
> since if my sent be good, I care not if
> It be as short as yours
>
> ('Life' 10–13, 16–18)

If death works like a mole to dig his grave ('Grace'), if the rebel cries 'Call in thy death's head there' ('The Collar'), in 'The Crosse' he uses the phrase taught to all in the Lord's Prayer and

---

Augustine and Aquinas. It is characteristic that the English Church was more concerned with what the Church did and wore in performing its worship; this is not trivial. The damnation of any individual could be known only to God, though the power of the keys was the priest's. Basil Hall thinks Perkins Augustinian.

used in the Agony in the Garden: '*Thy will be done!*'

Two images for the Flesh reflecting the conflict are the rose (familiar) and the box (idiosyncratic). The brilliance of the rose is dangerous, like the high complexion of the tubercular subject. The box encloses something precious; as the body, the soul. These two are brought together in one of the greater poems, 'Vertue', where the title recalls also Edward Herbert's plastic virtue. This late poem seems to enclose past, present and future so that time finally is transformed. A closer look here may end this survey of Herbert's ground.

> Sweet day, so cool, so calm, so bright,
> The bridall of the earth and skie . . .

The scene is a wide plain where earth and sky reflect each other, it is the great dominating Cambridge skyscape (or perhaps Salisbury plain) where the bridal is shewn in the ring that, all round, joins the two together.

> The dew shall weep thy fall to night;
> For thou must die.

Versicle and response end in a deep chime like a clock striking the hour. Except for the keywords, *bridal* and *to night*, it is monosyllabic.

The brilliance of the fiery rose (*angry* also means inflamed, when used of flesh) draws the gazer who suddenly finds it is himself that is weeping, for the hue speaks of mortality. So, in *Church-rents and Schismes*, had the Body of Christ, the Church, appeared. The pattern of the verse is now set, and the box of sweets, the lovely concentration of spring blossom, becomes one large tomb: and many springs are being recalled. All . . .

> My musick shows ye have your closes,
> And all must die.

Yet the harmony modulates; this is *not* the close. It moves from funereal spondees, tolling monosyllables, to an ampler ease, a transformation:

> Onely a sweet and vertuous soul,
> Like season'd timber, never gives;
> But though the whole world turn to coal,
> Then chiefly lives.

Plastic virtue revives in the vegetable form, the timber, that is now not the box, but the soul itself. Moving out of the blossoming Maytime, under the great roof of seasoned timber, the hundred oaks from Charlwood Forest given by King Henry VII, we see above no longer the embracing sky, but that glory of Cambridge, the roof of Great St Mary's. We have entered the Temple.

The great roof is seen at its grandest at the West Door, from Regent's Walk, the entrance still used in University processions, where the Orator would walk carrying his book and his lamp under the delicate stone tracery of the chancel arch that is like a little rose garden in stone, to the choir.

This may have been written in Wiltshire, but it is best brought to life in Great St Mary's—which was not only the University Church, but its Senate House and Examination School. As he worked to complete *The Temple* and *The Country Parson*, Herbert would have hoped in them to discern the way to continue in his pastoral office, to extend it beyond the ever-shortening number of his mortal days. In this way, as in 'The Water-Course', he turned afflictions to account. If

> No scrue, no piercer can
> Into a piece of timber work and winde,
> As Gods afflictions into man
>   ('Confession', 7–9)

winding into the 'box', even into its secret drawer—yet by avoiding 'fiction'

I challenge here the brightest day,
The clearest diamond

('Confession', 28–9).

Even at the Day of Judgment, both Temples still stand.

V

Henry Vaughan and the Poetry of Vision

RACHEL TRICKETT

CRITICS frequently disagree over the landscape of Vaughan's poetry; whether it is recognizable as that of the Usk valley where he spent most of his life, or is rather a landscape of the mind, emblematic and bearing little relation to natural description. F. E. Hutchinson in his *Life*, and E. C. Pettet in *Of Paradise and Light*, both take it as an instance of Vaughan's uniqueness in his age that he possesses a topographical quality. John Dixon Hunt in *The Figure of the Landscape*, on the other hand, takes precisely the opposite point of view, and Barbara Lewalski in her chapter on Vaughan in *Protestant Poetics and the Seventeenth-Century Religious Lyric,* is so determined to pursue Vaughan's use of the image of pilgrimage to its scriptural and theological sources, that you would think any simple association of the natural objects encountered on the way with those among which Vaughan actually lived, almost too naively superficial.

For all this, there can be little doubt that Hutchinson and Pettet are right. Vaughan thought of himself as the poet of a particular place. 'To the River Isca' is only the best and the best-known of several allusions to his native place in *Olor Iscanus*:

> CAMBRIA *me genuit*, patulis *ubi* vallibus *errans*
> *Subjacet* aeriis montibus ISCA pater . . .
>
> ('*Ad Posteros*'),[1]

---

[1] Unless otherwise noted, all quotations from Vaughan refer to the edition by Alan Rudrum in the Penguin English Poets Series (Harmondsworth, 1976).

and the volume itself is prefaced by this adaptation of Virgil:

> O quis me gelidis in vallibus ISCAE
> Sistat, et ingenti ramorum protegat umbra!

In his final publication, Thalia Rediviva, the elegiac eclogue 'Daphnis', commemorating the death of Thomas Vaughan his twin brother, refers again to the beloved river:

> So where swift Isca from our lofty hills
> With loud farewells descends, and foaming fills
> A wider channel, like some great port-vein,
> With large rich streams to feed the humble plain.
>
> (43–6)

At the same time, conventional though the topics and images of Vaughan's poems are, the showers, storms, springs, water-falls, stars, groves and seasons of his meditations, they are all observed with peculiarly intense physical, as well as imaginative, vision.

Take, as an example, Vaughan's water imagery. It is remarkably detailed and returns to the observed river again and again; the falls, the eddying water tinged with foam, the rapid flow, the spreading out into a wider channel which Vaughan described in 'Daphnis' as the Usk's especial features, are recurrent figures in his work:

> But as this restless, vocal spring
> All day, and night doth run, and sing,
> And though here born, yet is acquainted
> Elsewhere, and flowing keeps untainted . . .
>
> ('The Dawning', 33–6)

> As waters here, headlong and loose
> The lower ground still chase, and choose,
> Where spreading all the way they seek
> And search out every hole, and creek.
>
> ('Misery', 9–12)

> My thoughts, like water which some stone doth start
> Did quit their troubled channel, and retire
> Unto the banks, where, storming at those bounds,
> They murmured sore . . .
>
> ('The Mutiny', 6–9)

The immensely detailed poem 'The Water-fall' is only the most elaborate of a series of such river images. One aspect of still or stagnant water also obviously fascinated him: the way in which mist is exhaled from its surface. Hutchinson has plausibly supposed that 'that drowsy lake' of 'The Shower (I)' may be Llangorse Pool, near to Vaughan's birthplace, since 'a hot mist would rise from a lowland lake in cultivated country, whereas most of the Welsh lakes are clear mountain tarns'.[2] Vaughan had evidently seen this phenomenon and been struck by it. He uses it outside 'The Storm' several times—in 'Isaac's Marriage' (53–62), in 'Disorder and Frailty' (31–45), and in 'The Tempest' (26). In each case it is seen as a type of the soul's imperfect aspiration to God and its dissolution into the rain or dew of tears. And in each case it is clear from the detail that Vaughan had closely observed the vapour he applies so effectively to his devotional theme.

Climate and weather play an important part in his work, sudden storms especially. He would have found the topic of a storm in Herbert's *The Temple*, but the only time the elder poet gives us the feeling of climate is when he writes, 'I once more smell the dew and rain'. By contrast Vaughan's poems are full of weather:

> Many fair *evenings*, many *flowers*
> Sweetened with rich and gentle showers
> Have I enjoyed, and down have run
> Many a fine and shining *sun*,
> But never till this happy hour
> Was blest with such an *evening-shower*!
>
> ('The Shower(I)', 5–10)

[2] F.E. Hutchinson, *Henry Vaughan*, a Life and Interpretation (Oxford, 1947), p. 23.

Abraham, 'the first believer' in 'Retirement (II), has pitched his tent

> Where he might view the boundless *sky*,
> With all those glorious *lights* on high,
> With flying *meteors, mists* and *showers,*
> Subjected *hills, trees, meads* and *flowers*.
>
> (7–10)

Joy is

> Another mirth, a mirth though overcast
> With clouds and rain, yet full as calm and fine
> As those *clear heights* which above tempests shine . . .
>
> ('Joy', 14–16)

a phenomenon only to be observed in hilly country. In 'The Tempest' Vaughan refers to a recent drought when saying how everything in nature can show to man 'himself, or something he should see':

> This late, long heat may his instruction be.
>
> (3)

And the Welsh climate must have given him occasion often to experience what he writes in *Son-days*: 'A gleam of glory, after six-days-showers'.

Important as it is to see a poet in the context of his age's thought and conventions, something of the peculiarity of his imagination may be neglected if we tie him too closely to his historical setting. Thus, to see Vaughan against his native landscape as much as against his times, may draw attention to some aspects of his work which are as important to their imaginative effect on readers as his indebtedness to Herbert, his use of Protestant poetics, or his addiction to emblem. The old comparison between Vaughan and Wordsworth still has some value, even though we have acquired a more sophisticated knowledge of the poetic conventions and the theology of

the seventeenth century than those who first made it. For it
continues to draw attention to certain aspects of their imagination which may properly be compared. Both of them write a
poetry of vision in which sight, the physical seeing of a local
landscape, can be realized as the necessary prelude to insight or
revelation, though the insight of each is inevitably distinct.
Neither Vaughan nor Wordsworth is a visionary poet of the
same sort as Traherne or Blake. But the landscapes of their
poems, like the mountainous rainy regions in which they
lived, are illuminated very deliberately by each poet with
various kinds of light, from the simplest—'all the sweetness of
a common dawn' or 'those faint beams in which this hill is
dressed, after the sun's remove', to the most intense and
supernatural, 'the light that never was on sea or land', the
dying of the light of sense 'in flashes that reveal the invisible
world', the 'great ring of pure and endless light', or 'bright
shoots of everlastingess'. For each poet the consciousness of
light has a peculiar importance.

Vaughan's vocabulary of light needs only to be compared to
his contemporaries' for us to realize what a very different poet
he is from them. Even in his early love poetry to Amoret there
is none of that tired gem imagery Cavalier lyrists inherited
from the Renaissance which at its worst produces a flashy
glitter and no feeling of genuine radiance.[3] The object illuminated in good metaphysical poetry—Donne's 'bracelet of
bright hair' for instance, or Marvell's 'hatching throstle's shin-

---

[3] A typical example might be these stanzas from Edward Benlowe's 'The
Sweetness of Retirement' (Benlowe, being a pastoral and devotional poet,
may well be compared with Vaughan):

> When early Phosphor lights from eastern bed
> The grey-eyed morn, with blushes red;
> When opal colours prank the orient tulip's head,
>
> Then walk we forth, where twinkling spangles shew,
> Entinselling like stars the dew,
> Where buds, like pearls, and where we leaves like em'ralds view.

See Saintsbury (ed.), *The Caroline Poets,* Oxford, 1905, Vol. I, P. 449.

ing eye' is brilliant and defined, but never suggestive of the play or movement of light. This is conspicuously lacking in Herbert, whose poems are full of the light items of devotional poetry, stars, sparks, flames, and all of them almost entirely static and emblematic.

The metaphysicals took a profound interest in the symbolic and philosophical implications of light and darkness, day and night, as Sir Thomas Browne indicates:

> Light that makes things seen, makes some things invisible; were it not for darkness and the shadow of the earth the noblest part of Creation had remained unseen and the Stars in heaven as invisible as on the fourth day when they were created above the Horizon with the sun or there was not an eye to behold them. The greatest mystery of Religion is expressed by adumbration and in the noblest part of Jewish types we find the Cherubims shadowing the Mercy-seat. Life itself is but the shadow of death, and souls departed but the shadows of the living. All things fall under this name. The Sun itself is but a dark Simulacrum, and light but the shadow of God.
>
> *(The Garden of Cyprus,* Chapter IV)[4]

Vaughan's poem 'The Night' might be set side by side with this passage, for they could be read as commentaries on each other as far as ideas go, yet what a different imaginative world we are in with Browne! Though furnished with so many paradoxes and phrased in such splendidly elaborate cadences that it seems richly-textured at once, it is an almost entirely unvisual world, a world in which the eye has nothing to do.

Similarly, the popularity of the shadow as a subject from Donne to Henry King is in complete contrast to the way Vaughan uses it; in them the shadow's relation to light and body are essential elements in an intellectual exercise, but it is not *seen* as a visible phenomenon. Indeed poems or prose passages on light, or objects of light, or lack of light, in this

---

[4] Sir Thomas Browne, 'The Garden of Cyprus', ch. IV, in *Religio Medici and other Works,* ed. L.C. Martin (Oxford, 1964), p. 167.

period are for the most part meditations on the aboriginal concepts of light and darkness in their actual and extended metaphorical meanings. No other seventeenth-century poet appears to create for us, as Vaughan does, a real world of sights and objects, illuminated with sunshafts and clouded with shadows, and all, like the play of light itself in the hilly land-scape of the Usk valley, various, broken and full of movement.

Vaughan's poems use as repeated images the natural shows associated with light—clouds, dews, rainbows, shadows, stars, moonlight, sunlight, and they are, of course, used emb-lematically and scripturally as his epigraphs often indicate. But they create over the whole spread of his work a strong sense of place and climate. This is something we never find in Traherne, for example. Traherne writes:

> Tis not the Object, but the Light
> That maketh Heaven; Tis a pure sight.
>   Felicity
> Appears to none but them that truly see.[5]

What is missing in Traherne is precisely the object; he is too absolutely fixed in heaven, in the purity of vision. The rich and varied landscape of Herefordshire in which he was reared and where he lived at various times in his life is equally absent from his poems and his meditations.

Revelation in Vaughan comes from its true source, the God both immanent and transcendent, who is present in his crea-tion and yet exists beyond it. His illumination shines through and suffuses the natural world so that it seems to glow from the objects themselves even if they are only 'masques and shadows'. Often these objects, though part of a conscious system of emblems, are curiously changed by this illumination into familiar particulars of the local scene. A good example is from 'they are all gone into the World of Light!', where the memory of the dead

[5] 'The Praeparation'. Wade ed. *The Poetical Works of Thomas Traherne* (1932), p. 13.

> glows and glitters in my cloudy breast
> Like stars upon some gloomy grove,
> Or those faint beams with which this hill is dressed,
> After the sun's remove.
>
> (5–8)

The movement here is from a state of mind to an immediate scene—precisely the opposite direction from that which became so popular with topographical poetry in the next age. (In *Grongar Hill*, for instance, a poem again celebrating the landscape of South Wales, Dyer depicts the scene first and draws from it appropriate moral reflections.) Later in his poem, Vaughan, meditating on death—'What mysteries do lie beyond thy dust;/Could man outlook that mark!'—makes another delicate transition to metaphor:

> He that hath found some fledged bird's nest, may know
>   At first sight, if the bird be flown;
> But what fair dell, or grove he sings in now,
>   That is to him unknown.
>
> (21–4)

And here again the metaphor *solidifies* into a recollection of the local, natural world. The final stanza of the poem seems to epitomize its whole intricate pattern of the interchangeable relations between theme and image, between fact and figure:

> Either disperse these mists, which blot and fill
>   My perspective (still) as they pass,
> Or else remove me hence unto that hill,
>   Where I shall need no glass.
>
> (37–40)

In this imagery from Corinthians, of seeing through a glass darkly, Vaughan conveys not only the traditional aspiration to the fullness of knowledge in union with God, but also a longing for the barriers between the inner and the outer world to disappear, between the world of insight and the world of

physical sight which shift and turn so subtly in their relationship to each other in his poetry. The insistent repetition of
words of seeing and looking makes Vaughan's 'world of light'
a dual one, a spiritual and a material world, so that however
distinct they are, he can move easily in his imagination from
one to the other, and the transitions from the longed-for
imagined world to the real natural world, from statement to
metaphor, are an essential part of the discourse of the poem.

The repertoire of natural objects and effects in Wordsworth's poetry is strikingly similar to Vaughan's: clouds,
reflecting dews, rainbows, raindrops, moonlight, sunlight,
starlight, movement and the noise of water. Some of his
best-known passages illustrate this:

> The rainbow comes and goes,
> And lovely is the rose,
> The moon does with delight
> Look round her when the heavens are bare,
> Waters on a starry night
> Are beautiful and fair . . .
> ('Ode on the Intimations of Immortality', 10–15)

> All things that love the sun are out of doors,
> The sky rejoices in the morning's birth,
> The grass is bright with raindrops;—on the moors
> The hare is running races in her mirth;
> And with her feet she from the plashy earth
> Raises a mist, that, glittering in the sun,
> Runs with her all the way wherever she doth run.
> ('Resolution and Independence', 8–14)

But for Wordsworth the process of revelation is a very different one from Vaughan's. Insight or perception is reached by an
accumulation of sense impressions, and it is as if the surface
forms disintegrate and undergo a kind of metamorphosis: the
lovely morning of 'Resolution and Independence' turns suddenly grey, from the pressure of a deeper apprehension.
Wordsworth tells us how as a child he had to hold on to

material objects to assure himself of their existence. As a poet, it was equally necessary to him to enumerate with laborious authenticity each particular of scene or circumstance as a prelude to the amount of illumination he attempts so often (and often in such strangely negative terms), to define. The 'obscure sense of possible sublimity', the mind 'working with a dim and undetermined sense/Of unknown modes of being', the moment when Imagination 'that awful power,/Rose from the mind's abyss', and which, in the difficult conclusion to Book V of *The Prelude* he attempts to follow through, are all parts of the mysterious, transforming process of poetic creation:

> Visionary Power
> Attends the motion of the viewless winds
> Embodied in the mystery of words:
> There darkness makes abode, and all the host
> Of shadowy things work endless changes: there
> As in a mansion like their former home
> Even forms and substances are circumfused
> By that transparent veil with light divine
> And, through the turnings intricate of verse,
> Present themselves as objects recognised,
> In flashes, and with glory not their own.
> (*The Prelude*, Bk. V, 595–605)

Here Wordsworth is trying to analyse what is perhaps not susceptible to analysis in the last resort—the imaginative process of seeing, transforming and transcribing, or verbalizing. The forms and substances are the essences of the 'substantial things' with which Wordsworth's poetry deals, and which remain, however changed, *idem et alter*, through the power of the creative process. And they are the phenomena of the natural world; the loved landscape.

Vaughan, of course, has no such concern with examining the creative process. He is only eager to examine states of soul; the 'deep but dazzling darkness' of 'The Night' is the excess of

God's brightness; he appeals to God, not to any self-generating poetic power, to 'brush me with thy light'. Vaughan's task is, perhaps, a simpler one, but within the changing spiritual climate of his poems we are continually returned to the various world of creatures, so lovingly itemized together with their use in 'Rules and Lessons':

> To heighten thy *devotions*, and keep low
> All mutinous thoughts, what business e'er thou hast
> Observe God in his works, here *fountains* flow,
> *Birds* sings, *beasts* feed, *fish* leap, and the *earth* stands fast;
>   Above are restless *motions*, running *lights*,
>   Vast circling *azure*, giddy *clouds*, days, nights.
>
> When *seasons* change, then lay before thine eyes
> His wondrous *method*; mark the various *scenes*
> In heaven; *hail, thunder, rain-bows, snow,* and *ice,*
> *Calms, tempest, light* and *darkness* by his means;
>   Thou canst not miss his praise; each *tree, herb, flower*
>   Are shadows of his *wisdom*, and his power.
>
>   (85–96)

He works within a rhetorical structure where the metamorphosizing process that so fascinated Wordsworth has been regulated into a system of analogies and formal figures. Yet the idea of light and its function in the natural world, of sight as a co-relative of insight, is imaginatively of profound importance to both. In 'To the River Isca', an early celebratory topographical poem, Vaughan had written:

> But *Isca*, whensoe'r these *shades* I see,
> And thy *loved arbours* must no more *know* me,
> When I am laid to *rest* hard by thy *streams*,
> And my *sun sets* where first it *sprung* in beams,
> I'll leav behind me such a *large, kind light*,
> As shall *redeem* thee from *oblivious night*.
>
>   (25–30)

Images of light and darkness are commonplace in complimen-
tary poems, but Vaughan uses them here with a peculiar,
almost obsessive intensity. It is impossible not to feel in reading him that he is a poet who has actually observed the play of
light over landscape, and has become as imaginatively haunted
by this property as by the movement and flow of the water of
his native river. Both carry wide imaginative implications
beyond the simple symbolic equivalents—grace, human life,
transience that they superficially represent. Their function in
Vaughan's poems could be said to act, in Wordsworth's
phrase, 'As objects recognized,/In flashes, and with glory not
their own.'

'The Water-fall' is perhaps the best example of this intricate
quality of implication. The cascade itself is both an emblem of
human life and a real waterfall throughout. It is almost impossible to disentangle the two strands in the opening paragraph
where the movement of the fall is so deliberately and delicately
imitated in the metre and vocabulary:

    With what deep murmurs through time's silent stealth
    Does thy transparent, cool and watery wealth
      Here flowing fall,
      And chide, and call,
    As if his liquid, loose retinue stayed
    Ling'ring, and were of this steep place afraid,
      The common pass
      Where, clear as glass,
      All must descend
      Not to an end;
    But quickened by this deep and rocky grave,
    Rise to a course more bright and brave.

                      (1–12)

The tone changes to a simpler exclamation and an almost
Wordsworthian directness in the recollection of the second
paragraph:

> Dear stream! dear bank; where often I
> Have sat, and pleased my pensive eye,
> Why, since each drop of thy quick store
> Runs thither, whence it flowed before,
> Should poor souls fear a shade or night,
> Who came (sure) from a sea of light?
>
> (12–18)

Vaughan's fascination with the movement of the water leads to a sense of perpetual return to the source which can at once receive a religious application. And this application is extended in the last section of the poem to the more obvious associations of the element—baptismal renewal and redemption. The conclusion disentangles the various strands of metaphor and actual seeing, till something *beyond* sight supersedes the physical imagery of the poem, as death releases the soul:

> As this loud brook's incessant fall
> In streaming rings restagnates all,
> Which reach by course the bank, and then
> Are no more seen, just so pass men.
> O my invisible estate,
> My glorious liberty, still late!
> Thou art the channel my soul seeks,
> Not this with cataracts and creeks.
>
> (33–40)

Vaughan had alluded before to the noise of the Usk ('this loud brook' is like the 'shrill spring' of 'Vanity and Spirit' and the 'restless, vocal spring' of 'The Dawning'), and its other qualities of rapid movement, eddying flow (restagnating all), its widening course, its creeks and inlets. But here even the familiar river is at last relinquished, as Vaughan's poetry of vision reaches out, ultimately, to an *invisible* estate. For him light itself, as Browne wrote, is but the shadow of God.

The vocabulary of 'The Water-fall' is especially characteristic of Vaughan. Neither he nor Wordsworth cares much for colour epithets (except for Vaughan's often noted use of green, the symbolic colour, and white the non-colour, which those who know Welsh tell us means happy and blessed also in that language). Both may be contrasted in this with Keats, or with Tennyson whose luxurious topography has nothing of their peculiar kind of vision. Vaughan limits his descriptive words to such as suggest the lively, lucent quality of the element—transparent, cool, liquid, clear, quick, streaming. By this economy he achieves an extraordinarily intense and effective descriptive effect which is to some extent illusory (since little has been described), just as the natural world itself is illusory in contrast to the world of paradise. A similar economy of language has often been remarked in Wordsworth's style. In each case this kind of poetry of vision, though so intimately associated with a familiar and local landscape, does not try to characterize such detail by the use of epithets; there is no 'loading every rift with ore' in them. Vaughan and Wordsworth *clarify* the world they depict almost as if they were imitating in language the function of light.

A clumsy congratulatory poem by N.W. of Jesus College (Nathaniel Williams), printed in *Thalia Rediviva*, suggests that Vaughan's contemporaries recognized his peculiarity in making so much of his own landscape.

> Where reverend bards of old have sate
> And sung the pleasant interludes of Fate,
> Thou takest the *hereditary shade*
> Which Nature's homely Art has made
> And then thou giv'st thy Muse her swing, and she
> Advances to the galaxy.

(1–6; italics mine)

The 'hereditary shade' of Nature's 'homely art', the local landscape in which Vaughan's family had lived for so long, is the means the poet uses to reach his vision. He appears remarkably early as a poet who can at one and the same time *see* his own landscape in sensitive visual terms, and use it as a paradigm of his true theme—eternity. The idea of 'the prayer of creatures' is Vaughan's justification of his love of the natural world; God has 'hid in these low things snares to gain his heart', and to turn man to his eternal destiny. Of course Vaughan was not alone in his time in his love of the creaturely world. Marvell shows as great a fascination with it, but 'Nature's mystic book' is a much less localized volume to him than to Vaughan. No one would claim to recognize the landscape of mid-Yorkshire from *Upon Appleton House*, exact though many of its naturalistic details are. Marvell is quite a different kind of poet from Vaughan, and neither landscape nor light play a very important part in his work. Though he shares many conventions of thought and belief with Vaughan, 'vision', seeing and seeing *beyond*, is not what interests Marvell.

I am suggesting in this essay a way of looking at poetry which is not historical or scholarly. Both these approaches are necessary; but in the last resort we read poetry which survives outside the classroom in a way that ignores chronological strait-jackets. It is a peculiarity of English poetry that some of it, major or minor, in any century, may seem to reflect a personal response to the landscape and climate of an island where the sense of boundary, limitation and locality is exceptionally strong, and where the effect of climate is various and unpredictable. Vaughan, though I am not suggesting that it is his main claim to survival, is a good example of this. And though he is in no sense so great a poet as Wordsworth, he can properly be compared with him for this reason as much as for his interest in the state of childhood, innocence and pre-existence, among the topics they share. My argument is strengthened rather than weakened by the fact that there seems to be no evidence that Wordsworth ever read Vaughan.

It is just as likely that the effect of climate and weather on a particular kind of landscape should affect the imagination of some poets as it obviously does of some painters. No one doubts the influence on Turner and Constable of the countryside and the climates they depict. They were fortunate in living at a time when what stimulated their imagination was already aesthetically and theoretically respectable. Wordsworth has been compared to both of them, and Ruskin in *Modern Painters*, that great defence of Turner which developed into a whole new system of aesthetics, prefaces the finished work with a passage from *The Excursion*. The poet Edmund Blunden has compared the effect of Vaughan's poetry with a Claude painting,[6] but this seems altogether too calm, expansive, generalized and idealized for the particular movement and variety of Vaughan's scene. Molly Mahood makes a more convincing comparison with Samuel Palmer,[7] though Palmer's rich and heavy, thickly-wooded and static landscapes represent a different vision and a different countryside from the Welsh poet's. But both Blunden and Mahood are right, surely, in recognizing the strong visual as well as visionary quality in Vaughan.

Some lines from a recent sonnet, 'Conscious Light', by the glass engraver Laurence Whistler, attempt to convey the act and art of seeing:

> One field beneath the flying sun grows bright,
> Seems held for recognition and let lapse.
> You'd say that field was being thought by light.
> Perhaps earth is what light reflects on, thinking
> This field—that clump—those cottages. Perhaps
> The dark areas live in the same mind,
> Only not thought, put by, patiently shrinking,
> Back into darkness, reconciled though blind.[8]

The last two and a half lines of the same poem seem to me to epitomize very vividly the odd relationship in this art between

---

[6] Edmund Blunden, *On the Poetry of Henry Vaughan* (1927), p. 41.
[7] M.M. Mahood, *Poetry and Humanism* (1950), p. 255.
[8] Laurence Whistler, *To Celebrate Her Living* (1967), p. 107.

the natural world, the fact, and the vision, one which I have
tried to examine in Vaughan and more briefly in Wordsworth:

> O glory explaining
> How heaven, for a flash, is fact more than we know;
> Now it translates us, now we are the meaning.

VI

Marvell's 'Upon the Death of the Lord Hastings'

MICHAEL GEARIN-TOSH

'LORD HASTINGS' has received little critical attention and is
scarcely known to the general reader. Yet it is an important
and beautiful poem, urgent, wide-ranging and rich in
Marvell's characteristic fusion of ambiguity and delicate feeling, his sharp eye for human limitations yet keen feeling for
vulnerability and suffering. The main difficulty for a modern
reader is the poem's historical and personal context, which I
shall try to recover. 'Lord Hastings' has also had a run of very
bad luck. It was dropped from the canon for two centuries:
published as part of *Lachrymae Musarum* in 1649, it was omitted
from the folio of Marvell's *Miscellaneous Poems* in 1681 and all
subsequent editions until Grosart restored it in 1872. Then,
when the poem won its first admirer, no less than William
Empson in *Seven Types of Ambiguity*, an unfortunate impression was created as Empson shortened his account for the
second edition of *Seven Types* and added a footnote—the only
such footnote in the book—which explained that it had
'seemed hard to make the points convincingly without evoca-
tive writing'. Perhaps, the reader felt, this amounted to
Empson saying he was now less sure of the poem. On another
matter, too, Empson has not helped 'Lord Hastings'. Towards
the end of his analysis in both versions, he observed that the
poem was 'in fact, early work'.[1] Whether because of Empson
or not, 'Lord Hastings' is still dismissed as prentice work even
in full-scale studies of Marvell.

---

[1] William Empson, *Seven Types of Ambiguity* (London, 1930), p. 217.

When 'Lord Hastings' was published in the autumn of 1649, Marvell was twenty-seven. His first publication, 'Ad Regem Carolum Parodia', had been twelve years earlier. I think we can assume 'Lord Hastings' was also written in 1649 since it springs directly and densely from its immediate context. Was this early for Marvell? We know so little about when Marvell wrote that it is impossible to know how his style developed. But it may be that Marvell was a masterly poet by 1649. If 'An Horatian Ode' is contemporary with Cromwell's departure for Scotland—and there is no point in ending the poem with the departure if Marvell was writing after the Scots had been subdued—this great poem was written only a year after 'Lord Hastings'. Further, Elsie Duncan-Jones has suggested 1646 as the date for 'To His Coy Mistress'.[2] Her argument is that 'ten years before the flood' wittily refers to the dating of the Flood as 1656 years after the creation, 1656 *anno mundi*. I wish to support this dating with the fact that the year would normally be printed as 1656 A.M. in the seventeenth century. Thus, as in many paintings of the time, Marvell's poem contains a playfully hidden date and the initials of this painterly poet: 1646 A[ndrew] M[arvell].

None of this is conclusive, but there are no grounds for balancing the probabilities in favour of 'Lord Hastings' being 'early work', especially if this is taken to mean work which scarcely merits attention. Objectively 'Lord Hastings' may be placed between the two poems which we can date before and after it', 'To Lovelace' and 'An Horatian Ode'. This is a suggestive grouping. The ease and witty banter of 'To Lovelace', with its distinct but subordinate gravity, has become in 'Lord Hastings' a midway point before the miraculous balancing of equal parts which is achieved in almost every line of 'An Horatian Ode'. And if 'Lord Hastings' is contrasted with 'An Horatian Ode', some of its inter-

---

[2] *T.L.S.* 5 December 1958, p. 705. For objections to 1646 v. Roger Sharrock, *T.L.S.* 16 January 1959, p. 33 (referring also to *T.L.S.* 31 October 1958, p. 625).

pretative difficulties are clear. Topical events are the direct subject of 'An Horatian Ode', but lie just behind the themes of 'Lord Hastings'; and the events of 'An Horatian Ode' are huge public occurrences while those of 'Lord Hastings' are private, although in my view not wholly so.

*

A fundamental question has not been asked about the historical context of 'Lord Hastings': why was the young man commemorated at all?

It was a lavish commemoration. He was accorded a volume of poems, *Lachrymae Musarum*, to which Herrick, Denham, Marvell, Cotton, the young Dryden and many lesser poets contributed. If *Iusta Eduardo King*, whose second part contains 'Lycidas', seems to be a comparison, it remains notable that King had achieved more than Hastings. He had been a success in his seven years as a fellow of Christ's; he had published poems; he was committed to becoming a parish priest; he behaved with unusual dignity and piety in the shipwreck. Lord Hastings, much younger at the time of his death (nineteen: King was twenty-five), seems to have achieved little. It is true that the circumstances of his death were remarkable: he died on the eve of his marriage. But this is not an insistent theme in *Lachrymae Musarum*. Hastings also came from a famous literary family. Donne wrote epistles to his grandmother,[3] and his mother was the daughter of Sir John Davies. Yet no other member of the family (in the seventeenth century) was commemorated with a collection of elegies.

[3] v. J. Yoklavich, 'Donne and the Countess of Huntingdon', *P.Q.* XLIII, 1964, pp. 283–8.

The clue to *Lachrymae Musarum* is its title-page:

LACHRYMAE MUSARUM;/*The Tears of*
the MUSES: /Exprest in/ELEGIES;/
WRITTEN/By divers persons of Nobility
and Worth,/Upon the death of the most hopefull,/
[BLACK BAND]/*Henry* LORD *Hastings,*/
[BLACK BAND]/Onely Sonn of the Right
Honourable/FERDINANDO Earl of
Huntingdon/Heir-generall of the high-born
Prince/GEORGE Duke of *Clarence,*/Brother
to/King EDWARD the fourth./*Collected and*
set forth by R.B./[Line]/Dignum laude virum
Musae vetant mori. Hor./[Line]/*London,*
Printed by *Tho. Newcomb.* 1649./

This is notably genealogical, even for a seventeenth-century title-page, and the direction in which the genealogy points is spelled out. It points unmistakably to the English royal family. Seen in the context of autumn 1649, when Charles I had been executed a few months before, the title-page is a muted declaration of royalist feeling. Its sentiment is that royal blood is worth commemorating even in its minor scions.

The people had not been able to mourn Charles I. Even at his burial, attended by only a dozen people, the Common Prayer rites were denied.[4] The few broadside elegies which appeared were anonymous[5] and their publication was dangerous[6]—as was the brilliantly contrived circulation of *Eikon Basilike* in tiny, concealable copies.[7]

I think Lord Hastings was mourned for the royalty he shared as well as for himself. It was oblique mourning and on a

[4] C.V. Wedgwood, *The Trial of Charles I* (London, 1964), pp. 204–5.
[5] *Thomason*, British Museum 669 f.13 (78), (87), 669 f.14 (22), (36), (41), etc.
[6] P.W. Thomas, *Sir John Berkenhead 1617-1679* (Oxford, 1969), p. 171.
[7] F.F. Madan, *A New Bibliography of the Eikon Basilike*, Oxford Bibliographical Society Pubs., N.S. III, 1949 (Oxford, 1950), p. 2 seq.

hugely reduced scale, although extended through publication: *Lachrymae Musarum* went into a second edition in 1650.

The title page of *Lachrymae Musarum* is followed by a leaf which contains a decoration. The four royal crowns of England, Scotland, Wales and France are displayed prominently, with their insignia. This must have echoed the King's propaganda since the same decoration was used extensively in royalist broadsides during the months before the execution.[8]

It was impossible for the family of Lord Hastings or anyone else to publish overt royalist propaganda in the tense atmosphere of 1649 without offending the government. The printing of *Eikon Basilike* amply demonstrates Cromwell's determination to suppress dissent—and the huge risks which royalists were prepared to take in defying him. Perhaps the respect due to death led the printer of *Lachrymae Musarum* to feel he could risk the decoration of the royal crowns. In other respects, the tone of the book is discreet. Charles I is mentioned by name only twice. One poet imagines Hastings 'Above in Majestie, neer *Charles* his Wain'.[9] This line is the conclusion of his poem. Edward Standish is more outspoken:

> They're Angels guard him; King of kings hath sent,
> Where's difference 'twixt a Jayl from Parliament
> Cease then to weep; for he and Angels sing
> Hallelujah in Heav'n, with *Charles* our King.[10]

If, as I think likely, the family turned Lord Hastings's funeral into a quietly symbolic occasion, it is worth noting that they were in dire financial straits at the time.[11] Lord Hastings's father, the Earl of Huntingdon, was actually in the Fleet for

---

[8] *Thomason*, 669 f.13 (77), (78), 669 f.14 (36), (40).

[9] J.B., *In Honour to the Great Memorial of the Right Honourable Henry Lord Hastings, deceased*, pp. 50–3.

[10] *An Elegie on the much-lamented death of the Lord Hastings*, pp. 70–1.

[11] H.M.C. *Sixth Report* (London, 1877), p. 211; H.M.C. *R.R. Hastings* IV, 351.

debt at some point in or around 1650.[12] He had incurred immense losses in the early 1640s as a result of the Irish rebellion,[13] and by 1649 the family 'chiefly depended' on the marriage portion of Lord Hastings' fiancée. In view of this poverty, it is significant that they took such pains to bury their son ceremoniously. I have not been able to leave Oxford and examine the Huntingdon family papers in the Henry E. Huntington library. But some of these were published in the four volumes of H.M.C. *R.R. Hastings MSS* and I have found further evidence. A bill in August 1649 for mourning goods supplied to the Earl includes 'A black mourning saddle for your lordship. A pair of black stirrups and leathers . . . A double girth with black buckles, best sort . . . A black bit, best sort . . . A black snaffle . . . A pair of black spurs etc.'[14] There was a procession in London, 'several coats of houses born inclusive, adorning the Herse'.[15] Publication made the proceedings more widely known. The tombstone was engraved and published[16]—not a very common occurrence—and Lord Hastings's grandmother, Lady Eleanor Douglas, published a tract in his honour, *Sion's Lamentation*.

What of the young man himself? Little is known about Lord Hastings. Lady Eleanor Douglas describes him as 'heretofore inclining to the Royal Party'.[17] I have a further scrap of information which must be used with caution since it is uncorroborated. A broadside in the Thomason collection states that Lord Hastings was actually present at the siege of Colchester,[18] the great event of the second civil war in 1648 at which Lord Loughborough, his uncle, was a leading figure. Loughborough, a notorious extremist, was named by Parliament in

[12] H.M.C. *R.R. Hastings* IV, 351.
[13] v. petition received by House of Lords 24 May 1642, H.M.C. *Fifth Report* (London, 1876), p. 25.
[14] H.M.C. *R.R. Hastings* I, p. 394.
[15] Lady Eleanor [Douglas], *Sions Lamentation* (London, 1649), p. 3.
[16] Phil. Kinder, *Epitaphium super Hen. baronem Hastings* (1649). Broadside.
[17] *Sions Lamentation*, p. 8.
[18] *Thomason*, 669 f.13 (6).

1648 as one of the seven 'grand delinquents' of England.[19] It is tempting to connect the Thomason broadside with a letter which Ireton wrote to Lord Hastings's mother in 1642 expressing suspicion of Loughborough's influence on her and her son.[20] If Lord Hastings was with Loughborough at Colchester, it was an extremely rash action for the heir to a famous but impoverished family. Yet what an instance of cavalier recklessness, and how it would win the hearts of Herrick, Denham, Cotton and the royalist poets!

Lachrymae Musarum does not tell us whether Lord Hastings was at Colchester, and the family would surely wish to play it down in public, however much they treasured the memory in private. The government dealt harshly with the leaders, executing Lord Capel and Sir Charles Lucas. Loughborough escaped from prison and was abroad with Charles II. There are, however, oblique references in Lachrymae Musarum which prove nothing but have more weight if Hastings was at the siege. Marchamont Needham actually compares Hastings with Capel, although the comparison is generalized through association with two other royalist victims:

> Tis HASTINGS, he that promis'd to appear
> What Strafford, Falkland and brave Capel were.[21]

Capel, however, is given pride of place in that couplet. Another poem associates Hastings with his uncle, Henry Loughborough, and his grandfather, another Henry, who was 'one of the foremost to espouse the Royal cause in Leicestershire':[22] 'Three loyal HENRIES, sprung from Huntingdon'.[23] Another poet exclaims 'But O Sydneian, O Blood-Royal Fate!': if not killed in battle like Sidney, the young man may

---

[19] Commons Journals VI, 73 (10 Nov. 1648); 96 (13 Dec. 1648) revoked as 'derogatory to Justice'.

[20] H.M.C. R.R. Hastings II, 83–4.

[21] M.N. On the untimely death of the Lord Hastings, pp. 81–5.

[22] Henry Nugent Bell, The Huntingdon Peerage (London, 1820), second edition 1821, p. 114.

[23] Tho. Pestellus filius, On Henry Lord Hastings, pp. 59–60.

have fought for his monarch.[24] And in Marvell's poem, Lord Hastings watches military exercises in heaven and is connected with laurels in 53–4.

Nothing can be proved. But if Lord Hastings was at the siege of Colchester, he would be an outstandingly apt vehicle for the symbolic use which was made of his death.

*

Where does this leave Marvell? Is *Lord Hastings* a royalist poem? Can we now accept the argument that Marvell was a firm royalist in the late 1640s, perhaps wrote 'Upon Villiers' and certainly 'Tom May's Death'? I think not. In a way typical of Marvell until 'The First Anniversary', 'Lord Hastings' takes back all that it seems to give.

The occasion was royalist and there is apparent cheer for royalist readers. Marvell gives a political loading to the conclusion of his paragraph on Lord Hastings's death:

> Therefore the democratic stars did rise
> And all that worth from hence did ostracize.
>
> (25–6)

As Peter Heylyn explained in the early 1640s, a democracy is the disordered form of a republic.[25] It was a favourite term of abuse with royalist propagandists in 1648–9 for Cromwell's régime[26]—hence Marchamont Needham's fierce and celebrated couplet in *Lachrymae Musarum*:[27]

> It is decreed, we must be drain'd (I see)
> Down to the dregs of a *Democracie*:

. Marvell's 'democratic stars' *rise* and this is also a political gibe: rise as stars do, and rise in rebellion.

---

[24] Thomas Pestel the Elder, *On the untimely death of Henry Lord Hastings*, pp. 19–21.

[25] [Peter Heylyn], *Augustus* (London, 1632), p. 2.

[26] *Thomason*, 669 f.13 (87), 669 f.14 (10).

[27] M.N. *On the untimely death of the Lord Hastings*, p. 81.

There may also be cheer for royalists in what I think is a subtle dig at Lord Hastings's father. In heaven, Hastings reads 'the Eternal Book'

> On which the happy names do stand enrolled;
> And gladly there can all his kindred claim,
> But most rejoices at his mother's name.
>
> (38–40)

Perhaps this is gallant and affectionate, but no more. The Ireton letter, however, which I have mentioned, suggests that Hastings was not close to his father. One contributor to *Lachrymae Musarum* goes so far as to refer to the Earl and Countess as '*Lucie* large-soul'd and *Ferdinand* the meek',[28] and certainly the Earl's petition to Parliament in November 1645—after the King's cause was lost—would scarcely endear him to those who admired Loughborough and Capel: 'he neither took Arms [for Charles I], nor gave Contribution, or joined to their Councils or Commissions, and though he was divers Times sent for to *Oxford* never went'.[29]

So far, so good, for a royalist—and if Marvell had moved directly from the 'democratic stars' of line 25 to the 'crystal palace' of line 32, 'Lord Hastings' would resemble the other poems of *Lachrymae Musarum* in the comforting assumption that heaven was firmly and balmily Stuart. Marvell, however, inserts an introductory simile:

> Yet as some prince that, for state jealousy,
> Secures his nearest and most loved ally,
> His thought with richest triumphs entertains
> And in the choicest pleasures charms his pains;
> So he, not banished hence but there confined,
> There better recreates his active mind.
>
> (27–32)

---

[28] Thomas Pestel the Elder, *On the untimely death of Henry Lord Hastings*, p. 91.
[29] *Journals of the House of Lords* VII, 675.

The syntax is as slippery as the prince, and plays its part in undermining any confidence in this heaven: Marvell is probably referring to the occasion when Philip of Castile was driven ashore in England by a storm and festively detained by his ally, Henry VII, until the Earl of Suffolk, whom Philip was protecting from Henry, was brought from Castile and incarcerated in the Tower:

> In the meane time King *Henrie* led his guests to London, where hee entertained them with great and stately feasts, and royall sports; and the prisoner being arrived, they had libertie to depart at their pleasures.

This quotation is from a history of Spain[30] written by the father of Sir Theodore Turquet de Mayerne whose daughter was Lord Hastings's fiancée. The entertainments are also mentioned by Bacon in his *History of King Henry VII*[31].

Marvell's simile was a particularly bold one for the occasion of the poem, since his readers would quickly think of Charles I's years of detention and confinement. His captors were usually gracious and considerate, at least until 1648, and made some pretence that the King was not being forced in any way. Marvell sharply reminds his readers that princes can be jailers as well as prisoners, and this is part of his disengagement from both sides: at one moment 'democratic' stars are to blame, now a 'prince' keeps Lord Hastings from us with all the elaborate flummery of court life masking the shabby debasement of 'love' by 'state jealousy'.

*

Empson found that there were grounds for hope in Marvell's vision of heaven, although he comes to them in a subtle way. He was particularly attracted by the lines in which the gods are delighted by Lord Hastings's presence:

---

[30] Lewis de Mayerne Turquet, *The Generall Historie of Spaine*, tr. Edward Grimeston (London, 1612), Bk 25, § 4, sig. Oooo v verso: the pagination is repetitive and erratic.

[31] *Works* (London, 1841), I, 789–90.

The gods themselves cannot their joy conceal
But draw their veils and their pure beams reveal;
Only they drooping Hymenaeus note
Who for sad purple tears his saffron coat,
And trails his torches through the starry hall
Reversed, at his darling's funeral.

(41–6)

Empson read this as, in part, a description of sunset with the stars becoming visible, and he found the description of Hymen too intense to suggest no more than the saffron colour of marriage being discarded for the purple robe of mourning:

> *Only* means from the point of view of the allegory 'the only thing that prevents their perfect rejoicing', but as a matter of nature-study only the brightest stars, and they not fully *unveiled*, can be there to *note* the solemn celebrations of the nightfall. The next line contrasts its active and vehement verb *tears* with the 'tears' of weeping, then pronounced the same way (and the *coats* of a sunset are indeed formed of its *tears*), with the inactive sorrow of *drooping*, with the ritual dignity of the mythological figure, and with the slow far-reaching gradations of the colour-changes in the sky. If the *saffron* and *purple nòted* by *stars* are indeed a sunset (we are not told so) there is another quieting influence from the sun's regularity; from a sense that he may safely *reverse* his operations (dangerous and extravagant as this seems with most sorts of *torch*) in that his setting is only the reversal of his rising; from a sense of order and perhaps of resurrection in the death of the hero.[32]

I find that 'a sense of order and perhaps of resurrection' are denied by the poem and that Marvell's aim is to paint a bleak and indifferent universe.

Marvell's play on 'tears' should also be seen as a preparation for the final movement of the poem:

[32] *Seven Types* (Second edition, London, 1947), p. 170.

And Aesculapius, who, ashamed and stern,
Himself at once condemneth, and Mayern
Like some sad chemist, who, prepared to reap
The golden harvest, sees his glasses leap.
For how immortal must their race have stood,
Had Mayern once been mixed with Hastings' blood!
How sweet and verdant would these laurels be,
Had they been planted on that balsam tree!
   But what could he, good man, although he bruised
All herbs, and them a thousand ways infused?
All he had tried, but all in vain he saw
And wept, as we, without redress or law.
For man, alas, is but the heaven's sport;
And art indeed is long, but life is short.

                                                                          (47–60)

Tears unite 'Lord Hastings', from the quest for pure water to provide 'a store/Of tears untouched' in the opening lines to the tears of Hymen and finally of Mayerne, Marvell, his fellow mourners in 1649 and, hopefully, us.

Mayerne is first seen with Aesculapius, 'ashamed and stern', in four lines which are as much an epicentre of the poem as the couplet about Hymen on which Empson concentrates.

Marvell possessed to a rare ·degree the ability to combine universal statements with elegant, topical, sometimes personal allusion which bestows grace and civility upon harsher truths. Mayerne had been painted by Rubens in 1631. In a stunning portrait, he is shown sitting in front of a life-size statue of Aesculapius. The idea was probably original in portraiture and came from Rubens. It surprised and flattered Mayerne, as is clear from his letter to the great painter: 'Si je ne me cognoissois moy mesme, je serois en danger de me picquer d'un peu de vaine gloire mais non pas jusques là que de croire que les ornements d'un Aesculape . . .'[33]

Rubens's intention was not only that of complimenting Mayerne. The doctor is painted with a shrewd, kindly, but

<hr/>

[33] Aug. Bouvier, 'Un portrait de Turquet de Mayerne', *Genava* 15, 1937, 201.

almost pained face, his long mouth held tight and the carriage of his head most alert—he seems about to strain forward. The Aesculapius is set in an austere and shadowed niche. Although the light which picks out Mayerne's face and hands is not harsh, there is enough chiaroscuro to suggest the darker sides of a doctor's work, and the finished portrait (now in the North Caroline Museum of Art, exhibited in London 1972–3) is notably less sunny and genial than the preliminary study in chalk with washes of ink and water colour, the head in oil, which is in the British Museum.[34]. The overall impression of the portrait is that Mayerne has profound knowledge of the body's pains and compassion for them, but also knows the limitations of his skill. As a type of god, Aesculapius could cure anyone and, indeed, restore the dead to life. But limitations were forced upon him by Jove: in some stories he is destroyed by lightning in case men escape death, in others he is made a star, in *The Faerie Queene* he is kept in hell and 'endlesse penance' for restoring Hippolytus to life (I,V,xlii,6). Aesculapius, therefore, enforces the sombre and realistic tone of Rubens's portrait.

Marvell's idea of associating Mayerne with the 'sad chemist' is very bold. Mayerne was a controversial figure. Born in Geneva in 1573, he moved to France and became court physician to Henri IV. But the faculty of Medicine in Paris expelled him, petitioning the King not to take his advice. Henri ignored them. Mayerne visited England and finally settled here in 1610. He became a physician to James I, Charles I and Cromwell. The Paris dispute was repeated in England: in both countries Mayerne was championing the introduction of new chemical cures, particularly mercury, and was bitterly opposed by traditional herbalists. His chemical studies were, in part, alchemical. He was fascinated by the alchemists' belief that the stone was a panacea, and his MSS notes show him entertaining the possibility that mercury possessed near-

[34] For *ricordo* and portrait see Oliver Millar, *The Age of Charles I* (London, 1972), pp. 41–2.

panacea qualities.[35] Marvell uses 'chemist' in both contemporary senses of *alchemist* (OED 1) and one who used chemical medicine.

Mayerne is progressively humiliated in these final lines. First Marvell takes the popular, indeed vulgar moment of comedy when the alchemist's glasses explode (49–50); then Mayerne is reduced to bruising herbs—and only herbs—in a desperate attempt to save his daughter's fiancé (55–6); finally, when all has failed, he weeps 'as we, without redress or law' (58). But the tone is not one of humiliation. Alchemists were much suspected and often despised at the time, despite notable exceptions.[36] But Marvell's alchemist is dignified by his association with Aesculapius. 'Sad' instantly sets him apart from the leering rogue of popular literature—the word is actually used of Aesculapius at *Faerie Queene* I,V,xxxvi,7. 'Prepared' suggests not only readiness but the arduous preparations and spiritual purity of the serious projector. 'Reap/The golden harvest' makes his work life-enchancing and natural. And there is a lingering delight in fine writing, even at the moment of dramatic crisis: Marvell's *leap* is a witty play upon the French for explode, *faire sauter*.

In the final paragraph of 'Lord Hastings', the gods seem to be left behind. This is Marvell's essential strategy and, as so often with major transitions in his poems, it is anticipated in the syntax. Who is like the 'sad chemist' in 47–50, Aesculapius or Mayerne? Where is the main verb of these four lines? How do the lines connect with 41–6? We cannot tell. But in this suspension of grammar and syntax, Mayerne takes over from Aesculapius just as he has supplanted the whole pantheon of the gods. And as Mayerne's special knowledge and hopes become futile, he is given the humble but infinitely dignified description: 'good man'. Empson's account of 41–6 as a sunset bears the implication that night has now come, a night without stars. The scene in heaven is like a huge Rubens vista: now

[35] British Museum *Sloane MSS.* 1183, 1185, 1186, 1621, 1622, 1984.
[36] George St. Bredwell in his preface to the 1633 edition of Gerard *Herball*, sig. i8r.

Marvell tightens his focus upon the great physician who is cruelly aware of defeat, and has no other relief than tears. Only now does Mayerne weep.

The alchemist of 49 is more than an occasional illustration brought in to reflect Mayerne's interests. Alchemy is one of the underlying themes of 'Lord Hastings' and this has not been noted. Alchemical references accompany the use of tears at every point until the destruction of alchemy with the 'leap' of the alembics in 50.

The first lines of 'Lord Hastings' are often felt to have what John Dixon Hunt calls 'some strain'[37]:

> Go, intercept some fountain in the vein,
> Whose virgin source yet never steeped the plain.
> Hastings is dead, and we must find a store
> Of tears untouched and never wept before.
> Go, stand betwixt the morning and the flowers,
> And, ere they fall, arrest the early showers.
> Hastings is dead; and we, disconsolate,
> With early tears must mourn his early fate.
>
> (1–8)

Alchemy began with a laborious quest for exceedingly pure water: 'that clear water sought for by many, found out by few . . . which is the Base of the Philosopher's Work'.[38] This is one of the resonances of Marvell's lines in addition to the obvious adaptation of classical topoi: the fountain of inspiration, images in elegies seen as tears. Also Marvell's formal almost choric movement, 'Go, intercept . . .' 'Go, stand . . .', creates two sections which mirror the basic rhythm of the alchemical process. In the first four lines the water moves up, in the second four the water moves down:

---

[37] John Dixon Hunt, *Andrew Marvell* (1978), p. 68.
[38] Jean d'Espagnet, *Arcanum* in [Arthur Dee] *Fasciculus Chemicus*, tr. by James Hasolle [i.e. Elias Ashmole] (London, 1650), p. 169. For authorship etc. v. *Elias Ashmole: his autobiographical and historical notes etc.*, ed. C.H. Josten, 5 vols (Oxford, 1966), I, 63.

In the work of the Stone the other Elements are circulated in the figure of Water, for the Earth is resolved into Water, wherein are the rest of the Elements; the water is Sublimated into Vapour, Vapour retreats into Water, and so by an unwearied circle, is the Water moved . . . until it abide fixed downwards . . .[39]

Alchemy is also present in the lines about Hymen. An alchemist could only follow the progress of his experiment by its different colours, and the final stages were marked by orange, also called saffron, followed by a 'ruddy, sanguine' colour, also called 'the darkish rednesse of blood'; the stone or 'golden harvest' was then formed:

The Meanes or demonstrative signs are Colours . . . the third is Orange colour, which is produced in the passage of the white to the red . . . and is as the morning with her safron-haire a fore-runner of the Sun. The fourth colour is ruddy and sanguine . . . for this once and in the end onely gives a certain hope of the harvest.[40]

The same author elsewhere refers to the orange stage as 'saffron'.[41] The alchemical implications of saffron and purple make Marvell's couplet wonderfully dramatic and intensely poignant. The two principal areas of reference tear the image in two, mirroring the tearing of the saffron coat. At one level we see the approaching penultimate moment in the long alchemical process, the moment which assures us that the miraculous stone is about to be formed. On the other level, however, Hymen takes off his festive coat of marriage for a mourning robe. Lord Hastings is dead. There is no panacea. The stone does not exist.

There are other alchemical references in 'Lord Hastings' such as the tree of life in 20, but I hope my reading of the poem

[39] *Arcanum*, p. 215. v. also J.B. Lambi, *A Revelation of the Secret Spirit*, tr. R.N.E. (London, 1623), p. 59.

[40] *Arcanum*, p. 246; pp. 204–7.

[41] *Arcanum*, p. 216.

is now clear. A reader who picked up the uses of alchemy in Marvell's contemporary, Henry Vaughan, would have no difficulty with these elements in 'Lord Hastings'. Marvell uses them, however, in a way which is contrary to Vaughan. Alchemy for Vaughan was an image and confirmation of God's workings in the universe, and when he finally renounced 'false magic' in 'The Importunate Fortune', it was because he experienced religious ecstasy:

> And my false *magic*, which I did believe,
> And mystic lies to *Saturn* I do give.
> My dark imaginations rest you there,
> This is your grave and superstitious sphere.
> Get up my disentangled soul, thy fire
> Is now refined and nothing left to tire
> Or clog thy wings. Now my auspicious flight
> Hath brought me to the *Empyrean* light.
>
> (71–8)

Marvell begins 'Lord Hastings' with an apparent lip service to the conventional idea that heaven has snatched Hastings away because he was good beyond his years:[42]

> Alas, his virtues did his death presage:
> Needs must he die that doth outrun his age.
>
> (9–10)

He gives this the sort of political slant which readers of *Lachrymae Musarum* appreciated by blaming the 'democratic stars'—but instantly counterpoises them with the 'prince' and his 'state jealousy'. The tension is not reconciled but left so that it undermines any confidence we might have in the huge

---

[42] A classical idea, v. e.g. Martial X. liii, which was commonly adopted in early seventeenth-century poetry. An instance close to Marvell is Walter Colman, 'Elegy upon the Marchioness of Winchester' in *La Dance Machabre* (1632), p. 70:

> They [the Fates] were mistaken in their count, I fear,
> And numbered every virtue for a year.

Rubens-like vista of heaven. This is then withdrawn at the moment when Hymen symbolically tears his coat and Aesculapius and Mayerne—likened to an alchemist in his moment of failure—take over the poem. There is no panacea in this world. We can have no confidence in there being another world, and certainly not a better one than this. At the end of a successful alchemy, according to the quotation I have given, the water is 'moved until it abide fixed downwards'. Here there are only tears, also fixed downwards:

> For man, alas, is but the heaven's sport;
> And art indeed is long, but life is short.

VII

'Lycidas': The Power of Art

JOHN CREASER

'Never was the loss of Friend so Elegantly lamented'
Edward Phillips

COMING to 'Lycidas' at the end of *Justa Edouardo King* is still a shock. In particular, after the brittle and modish conceits of John Cleveland and others in the English section of the volume, 'Lycidas' seems a splendid anachronism, a three-masted barque under full sail among buzzing outboard motors. Why did Milton choose the unfashionable form of pastoral elegy for such a fashionable gathering of wits, especially if, as some believe, the volume was to some extent planned and shaped as a whole?[1]

Pastoral freed Milton from his co-authors' relentless spurts of wit,

> such elegies
> As that our tears shall seem the Irish seas,
> We floating Ilands, living Hebrides,

as Cleveland put it. Milton had played that game when Hobson died, and now the last thing he wanted was the narcissism of such 'tears in tune'. Indeed, what pastoral most offered him was something very different: a celebration of fellowship and community. The idyllic state which pastoral embodies is

---

[1] Michael Lloyd, '*Justa Edouardo King*', *N & Q*, 203, N.S. 5 (1958), 432–4. For a sceptical view, see Alberta T. Turner, 'Milton and the Convention of the Academic Miscellanies', *YES*, 5 (1975), 86–93, who also points out how small the trickle of pastoral elegies was in such miscellanies, although the trickle did continue beyond 1638.

communicated not so much by the shepherds' singing as by
their shared delight in song. The seminal seventh Idyll of
Theocritus has so rich a sense of felicity because the friendship
of man matches the abundance of nature. The responsibilities
of pastoral shepherds are light, and the easy task of caring for
their sheep only emphasizes their delicious *otium*; theirs is a
world which can be devoted to elaborate creation—whether of
songs, beechen bowls or oaten pipes—and the crown of their
relish of creation comes in the interchange of what has been
made. Competition is genial, and 'flyting' is without malice.
The shepherds delight in their shared attachments to a place
and to a traditional way of life which is in harmony with
nature. Even their names are traditional. As Schiller perceived,
pastoral is in its essentials 'the state to which civilization
aspires, as to its last end'.[2]

Being the nostalgic creation of urban sophisticates, pastoral
acknowledges its own simplifications, and is, of course, not
purely idyllic. Bucolic life is from time to time disturbed by
frustrated love, by death, or, as in Virgil's first Eclogue, by
tremors from the outside world. But this only enhances what
is under threat, since it brings its value to full consciousness:

> *fortunate senex, hinc inter flumina nota*
> *et fontes sacros frigus captabis opacum.*[3]

Milton concentrates on pastoral's vision of community not
only because of its appropriateness to a college's commemoration of a lost son, but because of his growing awareness of
'foul contagion' disrupting the community of England in the
1630s.[4] He does not so much assert a personal sense of loss out

---

[2] 'On Simple and Sentimental Poetry', *Essays Aesthetical and Philosophical*
(London: George Bell, 1875), p. 313. Cited in Lionel Trilling, *Beyond Culture*
(Harmondsworth: Penguin, 1967), p. 58.

[3] 'Happy old man! Here, amid familiar streams and sacred springs, you
shall court the cooling shade.' Virgil, *Eclogues*, I, 51–2 (hereafter cited as *Ecl.*).
Translations here and subsequently from the revised Loeb Classical Library
edition of H. Rushton Fairclough.

[4] Milton's own awareness of the importance of a congenial community is
clear in a letter to Diodati probably written in the same month as 'Lycidas'
(Yale *Prose Works*, I, 327).

of what Edward Phillips was to call 'a particular Friendship and Intimacy' with Edward King,[5] as he was to do later for Charles Diodati. Instead, he presents his share of communal grief at such a loss. For example, he does not make the familiar pastoral claim to enduring emotions so strong that sorrow will last until deer fly and fish forget to swim.[6] The loss is general, to 'shepherd's ear' not just his own. Lycidas is denied to 'our' moist vows, and the Church and university both join his mourning.

The events of 'Lycidas' are all in the mind's eye. It is a lonely poem of fellowship lost, and Milton's apprehension of pastoral fellowship has sometimes been misunderstood. E.M.W. Tillyard and others[7] have found egotism and self-pity in:

> So may some gentle muse
> With lucky words favour my destined urn,
> And as he passes, turn
> And bid fair peace be to my sable shroud.
> For we were nursed upon the self-same hill . . .

Instead, this has a beautiful allegiance to pastoral continuities. Poet has served singer and poet in song since Theocritus commemorated Daphnis and Virgil spoke up for Gallus. As Moschus for Bion, Anisio for Pontano, Spenser for Sidney, so Milton for King. The last act of pastoral fellowship and exchange is the creation of a memorial which will perpetuate the memory of the dead,[8] an act which invites and anticipates the continuation of that fellowship in generations to come.

[5] Helen Darbishire, ed., *The Early Lives of Milton* (London: Constable, 1932), p. 54.
[6] See, for example, *Ecl*. I, 59–63; Nemesianus, *Eclogues*, I, 75–80 (reprinted in Thomas Perrin Harrison Jr. and Harry Joshua Leon, *The Pastoral Elegy: An Anthology* [Austin: University of Texas Press, 1939], pp. 53–4); William Gager, *Daphnis*, translated in Watson Kirkconnell, *Awake the Courteous Echo* (Toronto and Buffalo: University of Toronto Press, 1973), pp. 224–5.
[7] C.A. Patrides, ed., *Milton's 'Lycidas': The Tradition and the Poem* (New York: Holt, Rinehart & Winston, 1961), pp. 58–63.
[8] See B.A. Wright, cited in J.B. Leishman, *Milton's Minor Poems* (London: Hutchinson, 1969), p. 273.

Milton's reference to his own death makes this understanding explicit. The lines are of remarkable equanimity; in neither case does the stress fall on 'my', whereas 'we', the word of relationship, must be strongly stressed.[9] Similarly, 'destined' quietly accepts that death will come when it will. Moreover, the poet's calm assumption of adequacy here supports those who take the shattered plants invoked in the opening lines to refer not to Milton's immaturity but to the premature death of King. There must be some self-concern in any mourning—it is the blight man was born for—but here the stress falls on the precious duty of commemoration: 'He must not float upon his watery bier/Unwept'.

The lines on the days when Lycidas and the poet were 'together both' continue to bring out the Johnson in some critics. J. B. Leishman objects to the fauns and satyrs because—unlike the rest here—they cannot be interpreted allegorically, while Eric Smith is embarrassed by the passage's emotion, since he cannot find what it refers to in the poem, the personal relation being suggested rather than described.[10] But *nothing* in the passage can be decoded in the literal-minded way of Johnson or Leishman: when Milton and King were undergraduates together, they must have been taking in sustenance, and were not in any important sense pastors. Other critics' attempts to find the original of 'old Damoetas' among various Cambridge tutors are equally misguided. The passage is an image of pastoral felicity. It alludes delightedly to earlier images of delight, to the *Arcades ambo* of Virgil (*Ecl.* VII, 4), to the fauns and others who respond to Virgil's singers (V, 72, VI, 27–8), and to the now pained recollection of shared youth in Castiglioni's great lament, *Alcon*.[11] The verbal echoes witness to pastoral's civilized continuity, its shared values and kindred

---

[9] Harrison, *op. cit.*, pp. iv and 18, twice italicizes the 'my' of line 20, remarkable acts of editorial *lèse-majesté*.

[10] Leishman, *op. cit.*, pp. 331–2; Eric Smith, *By Mourning Tongues: Studies in English Elegy* (Ipswich: Boydell Press, & Totowa, N.J.: Rowan & Littlefield, 1977), p. 25.

[11] See especially lines 78–82 (Harrison, *op. cit.*, p. 115): *Nos etenim a teneris simul usque huc viximus annis . . .*

spirits. Leishman also objects to the loose syntax of

> . . . and both together heard
> What time the grey-fly winds her sultry horn,
> Battening our flocks with the fresh dews of night,
> Oft till the star . . .

and suggests a tidier, 'improved' version (pp. 317–18). But the present participles ('opening', 'battening', 'westering') and the vague syntax convey a sense of time slipping delightedly by.[12] Meanwhile, the music almost seems to sing itself; 'the rural ditties were not mute'; fauns and satyrs 'from the glad sound would not be absent long'. But the lines end with a now poignant image of companionship: 'And old Damoetas loved to hear our song'. Their music-making blends into one song, its youthful promise as enchanting to the old shepherd as it is invigorating to the rough satyrs.[13] The first direct address to Lycidas follows almost inevitably: 'But O the heavy change, now thou art gone'.

Some of the piquancy of the verse does, of course, come from the sense that common experience and aspirations in real life lie behind it. But pastoral's way is not to insist on the real but to relish what has been made of the source in the real (as listeners relish what composers make of Paganini's pernickety tune). Here in Milton the sense of loss validates the idealization, while Johnsonian common sense kills the image's sense of 'play'.

Milton's stress on pastoral community leads him to a diminution of the tradition's magical elements. Fauns and satyrs dance to the friends' music, whereas in Virgil the

[12] Compare Rosemond Tuve, *Images & Themes in Five Poems by Milton* (Cambridge, Mass.: Harvard University Press, & London: Oxford University Press, 1957), p. 92, on this passage as 'life without time'. Isabel G. MacCaffrey, 'Lycidas: The Poet in a Landscape', *The Lyric and Dramatic Milton: Selected Papers from the English Institute*, ed. Joseph H. Summers (New York & London: Columbia University Press, 1965), p. 75, aptly compares *The Winter's Tale* I, ii, 62–5.

[13] The point is valid even if one's view of Damoetas is coloured by Sidney's *Arcadia*.

dancers are fauns and wild beasts, and even oak-trees nod their heads:

> tum vero in numerum Faunosque ferasque videres
> ludere, tum rigidas motare cacumina quercus.
>
> (Ecl. VI, 27–8)

For two thousand years the death of a singer had blighted nature. The sheep neither feed nor drink, wolves and lions howl, flowers droop and thorns flourish, laurels and tamarisks weep, mountains and rivers grieve, milk and honey dry up. This 'living continuity in the fabric of all created things'[14] is strikingly attenuated by Milton, and, as others have noted, nature's mourning virtually becomes a projection of human grief. Echoes mourn because Lycidas is silent. Trees will 'no more be *seen*' fanning their leaves joyously, yet their bliss may not have been violated. Canker, taint-worm and frost become items in a formal simile for human grief: 'Such, Lycidas, thy loss to shepherd's ear'. If sheep are hungry, it is because they are not fed properly by their pastors. The mourning of the flowers is entirely in the mind's eye, and is 'false surmise'.

Milton had perhaps sensed a contradiction within pastoral. Ruskin's harsh term, 'pathetic fallacy', is not entirely inappropriate, for at least since the Lament for Bion the bitterness of man's separation from nature's cyclic renewal had been insisted upon: mallows and parsley die and rise again, but we, however wise and strong, sleep in the earth for ever.[15] A further development of the pathetic fallacy—the assertion that the lamented singer had Orphic powers over nature—is not denied explicitly by Milton but is emphatically excluded in his insistence on the human frailty of even the archetypal poet, son

---

[14] Tuve, op. cit., p. 95. Her most distinguished account of the poem is weakened only by her refusal to acknowledge that Milton perceives some falsity in the 'pathetic fallacy'.

[15] Moschus, Lament for Bion, 99 ff. (Harrison, p. 39). Examples in other key elegies include: Sannazaro, Eclogues, XI, 55–63, and Castiglioni, Alcon, 55–64 (Harrison, pp. 101 & 114).

of the muse.[16] Words which could charm beasts and trees are helpless before the wordless and hence sub-human 'roar' of the mob. Indeed, the poet in 'Lycidas' is a classical 'maker' rather than a mage. However 'glad' the sound of their old music before the 'heavy change', even Lycidas himself had to 'build' the lofty rhyme, and the 'thankless muse' is a hard task-mistress.

Milton's diminution of the magical, with his stress on the 'uncessant care' which in reality is demanded by composition, leads to what I see as the second major reason for his choice of form. The pastoral elegy may not necessitate but it certainly encourages a high degree of poetic self-consciousness. Its traditional apparatus of muses and nymphs, and its time-honoured motifs and conventions, tend to make it a highly artificial form, so that the reader is unusually aware that he is reading a poem, a *work* of art which must be seen in the light of a tradition. And no pastoral elegy is so explicitly artificial as 'Lycidas', with its numerous invocations and apostrophes, its ostentatious digressiveness and variation of tone ('that strain I heard was of a higher mood'), and its deliberate exercise in the ancient topoi. This cannot but lead to the challenge so dogmatically posed by Johnson: 'Where there is leisure for fiction there is little grief'. No poem of medium length has been as celebrated as 'Lycidas', yet these words of Johnson continue to nag.

They nag because—in speaking up for 'the power of art without the show' which his own elegy on Dr Robert Levet so finely manifests—Johnson anticipates post-Romantic assumptions favouring sincerity and spontaneity, and, less predictably, anticipates the older New Criticism's version of this presupposition. T.S. Eliot said that his aim was 'to write poetry which should be essentially poetry, with nothing poetic about it, . . . a poetry so transparent that we should not see the poetry but that which we are meant to see through the

---

[16] For examples, see Petrarch, *Aegloga*, II, 110–11, and Alamanni, *Eclogues*, I, 21 ff. (Harrison, pp. 70 & 121), and William Gager (Kirkconnell, *op. cit.*, p. 223).

poetry.'[17] For Eliot, Milton's far from self-effacing idiom could become 'a solemn game'.[18] The nub of F.R. Leavis's attempted 'dislodgement' of Milton was that 'he exhibits a feeling *for* words rather than a capacity for feeling *through* words',[19] and he commented harshly on 'Lycidas' in passing. A less principled disdain for the obtrusive medium of the poem is found in other distinguished men of letters: for Robert Graves the poem is 'strangled by art', while for W.H. Auden the poem is beautiful only if read as nonsense-verse, where it is as irrelevant to ask 'Who is the Pilot of the Galilean Lake?' as it is to ask 'Who is the Pobble who has no toes?'[20]

Nevertheless, the poem continues to exercise its power to move and console, as is manifest in the deeply responsive quality of the finest recent criticism,[21] and also most poignantly captured in John Berryman's short story, 'Wash Far Away', where a still young but jaded teacher, mourning the loss of his closest friend, is warmed back towards life when led to see the poem with new eyes.[22]

That there is passion in the poem hardly requires demon-

---

[17] Cited by Enid Starkie, *From Gautier to Eliot* (London: Hutchinson 1960), p. 165.

[18] John Hayward, ed., *T.S. Eliot: Selected Prose* (Harmondsworth: Penguin, 1963), p. 123.

[19] F.R. Leavis, *Revaluation: Tradition and Development in English Poetry* (1936; rpt. Harmondsworth: Penguin, 1964), p. 48.

[20] Robert Graves, *The Crowning Privilege* (Harmondsworth: Penguin, 1959), p. 341; W.H. Auden, *The Dyer's Hand and Other Essays* (London: Faber, 1963), pp. 340–1.

[21] Especially Ellen Zetzel Lambert, '*Lycidas*: Finding the Time and the Place', *Placing Sorrow* (Chapel Hill: University of North Carolina Press, 1976), pp. 154–86. Other distinguished recent studies include: Paul Alpers, 'The Eclogue Tradition and the Nature of Pastoral', *CE*, 34 (1972), 352–71; MacCaffrey, *art. cit.*; Louis L. Martz. '*Lycidas*: Building the Lofty Rhyme', *Poet of Exile: A Study of Milton's Poetry* (New Haven & London: Yale University Press, 1980), pp. 60–75; Eugene Paul Nassar, '*Lycidas* as Pastiche', *The Rape of Cinderella: Essays in Literary Continuity* (Bloomington & London: Indiana University Press, 1970), pp. 16–27; Balachandra Rajan, '*Lycidas*: The Shattering of the Leaves', *The Lofty Rhyme: A Study of Milton's Major Poetry* (London: Routledge, 1970), pp. 45–55.

[22] John Berryman, *The Freedom of the Poet* (New York: Farrar, Straus & Giroux, 1976), pp. 367–86.

stration now. In re-writing the lines on Orpheus, Milton struck out the softening sentimentalities of 'the golden hayrd Calliope' and 'the gods farre sighted bee' in order to stress the impotence of even 'the muse herself'. There is a chilling sense of human frailty when the blind Fury 'slits the thin-spun life', or when 'the remorseless deep/Closed o'er the head'—the sea, malignant and predatory, seems at once to send its victim irretrievably to the depths.

Why, then, did Milton choose to write a passionate poem with so much 'show', and what, if anything, did he gain by it? At first the 'show' may seem to offer only the rewards of connoisseurship to a 'fit audience'—the pleasures of recognizing both the familiar and the new—rewards which are not to be underestimated but which may seem minor from a poem of such passion on such a subject.

It is not simply that Milton uses, and adapts, the motifs of earlier writers: the helpless appeal to absent nymphs, the train of mourners, the apotheosis of the lost one, the departure from the fields at sunset, and many besides. The more one re-reads his predecessors, the more one realizes how fully he had made a great tradition his own. What is striking, however, is the exquisite felicity with which Milton re-creates the hallowed commonplaces:

> For Lycidas is dead, dead ere his prime,
> Young Lycidas, and hath not left his peer.
> Who would not sing for Lycidas?

The rapt reiteration of the beloved name echoes Virgil:

> *nos tamen haec quocumque modo tibi nostra vicissim*
> *dicemus, Daphnimque tuum tollemus ad astra;*
> *Daphnim ad astra feremus: amavit nos quoque Daphnis.*[23]

---

[23] *Ecl.* v, 50–3 ('Still I will sing you in turn, poorly it may be, this strain of mine, and exalt your Daphnis to the stars. Daphnis I will exalt to the stars; me, too, Daphnis loved.').

and Castiglioni:

> *Alcon deliciae Musarum et Apollinis, Alcon*
> *Pars animae, cordis pars Alcon maxima nostri,*
> *Et dolor . . .* [24]

and Spenser:

> Young Astrophel, the pride of shepherds' praise,
> Young Astrophel, the rustic lasses' love. [25]

as well, of course, as recalling Virgil's *neget quis carmina Gallo*? (*Ecl.* X, 3). It is not, as E.K. put it, that 'walking in the sun . . . needs he mought be sunburnt; and, having the sound of those ancient poets still ringing in his ears, he mought needs, in singing, hit out some of their tunes'. Milton's lines are a conscious act of homage to a tradition, and perform for that tradition the supreme service of renewing rather than imitating it. The eloquent poise of Milton more than matches that of his great predecessors. The first line balances, with poignant formality, around the repeated word 'dead'. Both must be heavily stressed, not only through meaning and sound, but because the first requires weight to offset the lightness with which the previous technically stressed syllable, '-das', is spoken, and because the second disrupts the iambic flow and, like the death itself, arrives prematurely. The first two lines balance one another, with 'his prime' and 'his peer' creating like endings, and with 'Lycidas' beginning twice in the second syllable, while the insertion of 'young' in the second line is more poignant, by restraint, than is the double use in Spenser. [26]

---

[24] *Alcon*, 24–6 ('Alcon, beloved of the Muses and of Apollo, Alcon, the half of my soul, Alcon, thou chief part of my heart and source of my grief . . .' Harrison, p. 113).

[25] *Astrophel*, 7–8. See also *November*, 37–8 & 56–9, and *The Faerie Queene* III. vi. 45.

[26] Or, for that matter, in Milton's own 'Fair Infant': 'Young Hyacinth born on Eurotas' strand,/Young Hyacinth the pride of Spartan land.'

Such writing (and my analysis could be extended into many passages) is an act of love. In lavishing such art upon inherited matter, Milton expresses his devotion to the traditional values of pastoral community, and so through that his sense of what the death of Lycidas means to the community.

But Milton does not, of course, simply assume pastoral modes and values:

> Return, Alphéus, the dread voice is past
> That shrunk thy streams; return, Sicilian muse.

Pastoral streams cease to flow either through sorrow at a singer's death or through delight in his singing: *et mutata suos requierunt flumina cursus.*[27] Milton's, however, shrink in dread before the supernatural voice. Through the unprecedented intrusion of ecclesiastical polemic into pastoral elegy, Milton uses pastoral means to indicate the limitations of pastoral.[28]

He is, therefore, using the self-consciousness of his form to heighten the reader's awareness of what is valuable and what is limited in pastoral. The poem is, however, more self-conscious still. More than most readers seem prepared to accept, the poem counters its ritualistic quality, while nevertheless insisting on its artifice, through deliberate verbal idiosyncrasy.[29] Despite the insistence of critics such as Thomas Kranidas that the doctrine of decorum in Milton—'the grand masterpiece to observe'—is not restrictive but a 'resonant principle of dynamic unity',[30] the pressure of language is such

[27] *Ecl.* VIII, 4: 'and rivers were changed and stayed their course'.
[28] James H. Hanford, 'The Pastoral Elegy and Milton's *Lycidas*', Patrides, *op. cit.*, p. 54. Mother Mary Christopher Pecheux, 'The Dread Voice in *Lycidas*', *Milton Studies*, 9 (1976), 221–41, argues on the basis of this passage that 'the pilot of the Galilean lake' must include Moses. But in Exod. 14: 21–2 Moses stretches out his hand without speaking, and the waters do not shrink but form two walls.
[29] Among editors, Dennis Burden, *The Shorter Poems of John Milton* (London: Heinemann, 1970), p. 149 *et seq.* is, to my knowledge, the exception proving the rule. He alone points to the frequent violence of the language, adding, 'Johnson was very right to call its diction "harsh".'
[30] *The Fierce Equation: A Study of Milton's Decorum* (The Hague: Mouton, 1965), p. 32.

that stress on his decorum tends to make him appear merely decorous. Critical unease with the term 'digression' is representative here. It is significant how often the splendid impertinence of the triumphant 'sun in bed' image in 'The Nativity Ode' is either censured or explained away. The same reactions are found—although less consistently—to the most bizarre image in 'Lycidas': 'Blind mouths! that scarce themselves know how to hold/A sheep-hook'. Ruskin's brilliant reading of 'blind mouths' in *Sesame and Lilies* has been accepted by almost all, but there is a desire to explain away 'mouths' as meaning, say, no more than 'spokesmen', for how could a mouth hold a sheep-hook?[31] Such a line of defence implies that Milton was of extraordinary verbal insensitivity. Instead, we must be prepared to read Milton with the flexibility of mind with which we approach the author of 'their daggers/Unmannerly breeched with gore', and 'Pity, like a naked new-born babe,/Striding the blast'. Milton is writing invective here and is hence less subtle than Shakespeare, but the very point of his image is its incongruity, since *nothing* could be adequate to the incongruity of these false pastors. Their utter disruption of the natural order is expressed in the bizarre bodily dislocations of the image.

But this line is only the extreme example of the poem's inventive idiosyncrasy. Milton draws attention to his language throughout, using several new words or words in new senses (for example, 'inwrought', 'scrannel', 'freaked', 'monstrous', 'sorrow', 'ore'), as well as many brief conceits, strikingly transferred epithets and unusually compressed expressions. It is a poem where the wind parches a body floating in the sea, where a tear is melodious, where the act of *turning* implies making a *verse*, where a fly has a 'sultry horn', where

---

[31] W.K. Thomas, 'Mouths and Eyes in *Lycidas*', *Milton Quarterly*, 9 (1975), 39–42; with an unilluminating reply by Wayne Shumaker, 10 (1976), 6–7. Archibald A. Hill, 'Imagery and Meaning: A Passage from Milton, and from Blake', *TSLL*, 51 (1969), 1093–1105, censures the passage in neo-neoclassical terms for mixing metaphors.

flocks fatten on dew, where the Fates are Furies,[32] where ears tremble, where rugged wings blow from beakéd promontories, where a flower is woeful yet in more than one sense 'sanguine', where a star is black, where eyes suck and can be thrown, where a pink is white and the jet of mourning flecks a flower capriciously, where shores wash a body far away, where the domain of sea-beasts seems to exemplify the whole 'monstrous world', where the ocean is at once a floor and a bed, and where the morning has opening eyelids and the sky a forehead. The expressions cited here (and the list could be extended greatly) are not, of course, mere freaks of wit, and all could be justified. The *fattening* of flocks on dew, for example, is a deft transcendence of the pastoral tradition that sheep find dewy grass the most delicious; since dew is traditionally associated with both manna and Christ, figuratively the green pastures into which the poet-pastors led their sheep would be those of the Gospel.[33] However, faced with so many such expressions, it is hardly adequate to argue, with Leishman, that Milton ruthlessly sacrificed or subdued 'conceited' phrases in the interests of decorum and unity of texture,[34] or even, with David Daiches, that 'paradoxes are subdued and woven completely into the texture'.[35]

It is true that much in the poem does its work almost subliminally. The texture is so rich that any devoted reader of 'Lycidas' can unravel significant nuances unnoted in the remarkably extensive literature on the poem. Why, for

[32] There is in fact a little classical precedent for the blending of Fates and Furies; Osgood cites Aeschylus, *Prometheus Bound*, 516. See also Hesiod, *Theogony*, 217–22.

[33] *Ecl.* VIII, 15, with *Georgics*, III, 326; *Comus*, 540–2; Exod. 16: 14–15; Numb. 11: 9; Marvell, 'On a Drop of Dew', 37–40; Vaughan, 'The Seed Growing Secretly', 4–8. Milton had been anticipated by Phineas Fletcher in naive lines which he obviously knew: 'Home then my lambes; the falling drops eschew;/Tomorrow shall ye feast in pastures new,/And with the rising sun banquet on pearled dew.' (*The Purple Island*, VI, 77).

[34] *Op. cit.*, p. 307 ff. Several of Leishman's examples, plus some of those he does not discuss, could easily be used against his case.

[35] Cited by A.S.P. Woodhouse & Douglas Bush, eds., *A Variorum Commentary . . . on the Minor English Poems* (London: Routledge, 1972), II, ii, 578.

example, does the strictly redundant word 'forehead' seem so triumphant when the sun 'flames in the forehead of the morning sky'? Clearly, 'flames' transcends the 'sudden blaze' and 'flashy' songs earlier, while the image as a whole, with superb confidence, rejects the Catullan tradition (shared, as mentioned above, by pastoral elegists such as Castiglioni and Sannazaro), that

> *soles occidere et redire possunt:*
> *nobis cum semel occidit brevis lux,*
> *nox est perpetua una dormienda.*

But 'forehead' cannot just be there for the alliteration. Throughout the poem, life has been epitomized with unusual frequency by the head or parts of the head. This stems naturally from the drowning ('That sunk so low that sacred head of thine'), but is used extensively to express not only man's physical but also his moral and emotional frailty: 'Such, Lycidas, thy loss to shepherd's ear'; 'His gory visage down the stream was sent'; 'To sport . . . with the tangles of Neaera's hair'; 'my trembling ears'; 'Blind mouths!' There is, then, great exhilaration in the reversal of such images as the sun 'repairs his drooping head', while the washing of the 'oozy locks' and wiping away of tears from his eyes for ever become ineffably touching. Conversely, the action of hands in the poem—'forced fingers rude', the shears, the 'two-handed engine'—takes on peculiar menace.

The poem is so finely wrought that even linguistic minutiae contribute to its effect. The indefinite article occurs only three times in the 193 lines.[36] Milton seems deliberately to avoid it at times ('some melodious tear'; 'the worthy bidden guest'), whereas the definite article is used even where it is not strictly needed ('Ye valleys low where the mild whispers use'), or where another turn of phrase might seem more predictable ('the rural ditties . . . the glad sound . . . '), or as a demonstra-

---

[36] In lines 87, 120 and 152 (excluding lines 97 and 135, where 'a' is equivalent to 'one').

tive ('Where the great vision of the guarded mount'). The frequent indefinite articles in the tentative opening of 'Samson Agonistes' make an instructive comparison. Euphony and rhythm must have influenced some choices in 'Lycidas', but the overall effect is to heighten uncertainty where the indefinite article is used ('a higher mood'; 'a sheep-hook'—*any* sheep-hook at all; 'a little ease'), and give extra weight to the demonstrative 'that': 'That last infirmity of noble mind'; 'that fatal and perfidious bark'; 'that two-handed engine'.

While 'Lycidas' could not give the impression of inexhaustible significance that it does without nuances such as these, the manifest artifice is equally vital, and is in more danger of under-estimation. This is clear from the current tendency to read 'Lycidas' as very much a *dramatic* poem. In several more extreme readings, the poem becomes a dramatic monologue almost in the Browning sense, where the key to the poem is the discrepancy between the character's *apologia pro vita sua* and the author's implied interpretation. In such readings, stress tends to fall on 'the uncouth swain' and his alleged paganism. The poem is turned topsy-turvy; it is read in the light of the abrupt emergence of the swain in the last stanza, and Milton's headnote ('In this monody the author bewails a learned friend') is ignored. Such readings face an immovable object in the vision of Lycidas in heaven, and this has to be explained away (quite without textual support) as the words of the archangel Michael, or as a fit of glossolalia, or as the dropping of a pagan mask, or as the revealingly self-indulgent choice of what is comforting rather than punitive in the Book of Revelation, and so on.[37]

[37] See, respectively, William G. Madsen, *From Shadowy Types to Truth: Studies in Milton's Symbolism* (New Haven and London: Yale University Press, 1968), p. 13 ff.: David Shelley Berkeley, *Inwrought with Figures Dim* (The Hague: Mouton, 1974), pp. 13, 31–2, 42, 44; Roberts W. French, 'Voice and Structure in *Lycidas*', *TSLL*, 12 (1970), 15–25; Emory Elliott, 'Milton's Uncouth Swain: The Speaker in *Lycidas*', John Karl Franson, ed., *Milton Reconsidered: Essays in Honor of Arthur E. Barker* (Elizabethan & Renaissance Studies, University of Salzburg, 1976), pp. 1–21. At least six other recent articles on these lines could be listed.

On the other hand, some of the most distinguished of recent critiques, notably those of Ellen Lambert, Isabel MacCaffrey and Eugene Nassar, see the poem less as a dramatic monologue than as a soliloquy, a groping after truth. For Nassar, for example, the poem 'flops and jumps and starts' and has 'immense impetuosity' (pp. 17–18). For MacCaffrey, the opening of the poem is brutally direct, and does not suggest how it will end (pp. 65–6). For Lambert, the poem is a gradual ebb and flow of discovery (pp. 156–7).

Such readings, however, underestimate the effect of what Balachandra Rajan has termed the 'significant symmetries' of the poem,[38] and of that intrusive sense of artifice which I have been discussing. These critics also seem to me to complicate the poem as a dramatic sequence. Remarkably little 'progress' has apparently been made when suddenly the great outburst 'Weep no more woeful shepherds' is heard. At the 'Ay me!' of line 154 the mourner is, if anything, deeper in delusion than he was at the 'Ay me!' of line 56. His reaction to Peter's speech is exactly what it was to Apollo's: to summon the sources of pastoral; the superhuman speakers are almost brushed aside. Furthermore, although Apollo juts dramatically into the poem with an unheralded speech (which, for the first time, begins a sentence in mid-line), he intrudes in the past tense: 'But not the praise,/Phoebus replied', and the sequence of mourners which culminates in Peter continues almost entirely in the past tense, even though the poet is listening in the present:

> But now my oat proceeds,
> And listens to the herald of the sea
> That came in Neptune's plea.
> He asked the waves . . .[39]

We have here less a process of discovery than a sense of blockage, a return to past rejections of enlightenment. Apollo

---

[38] *Op. cit.*, p. 53. Rajan has perhaps a finer sense than other critics that the poem has both 'the *brio* of performance' and a 'perilous openness' (p. 55).

[39] On tenses in the poem, see Lowry Nelson Jr., *Baroque Lyric Poetry* (New Haven and London: Yale University Press, 1961), pp. 64–76.

and Peter offer ultimate rather than immediate solutions, and the trust in providence which they require cannot satisfy the mourner. This remains a dramatic way of seeing the poem, of course, but less one of tentative, gradual discovery than has been suggested. Any process of discovery must be concentrated in the lines which immediately precede the great exclamation, 'Weep no more . . .'

The critical problem here is acute, because, at least in their primary statement, these lines lead, as Cleanth Brooks and John Edward Hardy say, to the nadir of despair.[40] The departure of St Peter leads to an attempt to find comfort in pastoral ceremony, only for this to be dismissed as 'false surmise'. It is acknowledged that the body of Lycidas may in fact be anywhere from Land's End to beyond the Hebrides. His plight is beyond help, and the archangel is implored to feel pity rather than to act. The only hope is that dolphins will at least bring the body to land (presumably so there can be a burial). The appeal to the dolphins is not an appeal for rescue—'hapless' precludes hope. The allusion here is less to particular stories of dolphins (such as their rescue of Arion) than to the ancient tradition of dolphins' friendliness to man and readiness to bring to land anyone found in the sea, whether dead or alive.[41] Commentators' stress on stories of miraculous rescue or divine intervention obscure the primary meaning here.

If the passage is so despairing, why do almost all readers find the abrupt reversal at 'Weep no more' deeply convincing (even though some intrude a new speaker here)?[42] In part, the reversal has to be sudden if it is to represent a flood of revelation, but Samson's equivalent 'rousing motions' flow naturally from

[40] 'Essays in Analysis: Lycidas', Patrides, op. cit., p. 150.

[41] See especially, Plutarch, Moralia, 984 C–D in modern editions or p. 979 in Philemon Holland's translation—Morals (London, 1603)—where the dolphin's love of man is related in a series of stories which involve dead and living men indifferently.

[42] Christopher Hill, Milton and the English Revolution (London & Boston: Faber, 1977), pp. 52 & 460, is exceptional in finding this passage 'perfunctory'. In studying this peripeteia, I have profited especially from the essays of Alpers, Lambert and Rajan cited above, and from John Reesing, Milton's Poetic Art (Cambridge, Mass.: Harvard University Press, 1968), p. 22 ff.

the regeneration of faith and confidence we have witnessed.

A major reason is that the despair in the sea passage is at least purged of 'false surmise'. To withdraw from the 'dread voice' of Peter to the streams of pastoral is here a form of self-delusion, and the haunting beauty of the floral passage only adds to this impression. It is indeed 'leisure for fiction', although only there because there is so much grief. Whereas the pastoral rite of decking the tomb is a communal act,[43] here the speaker is solitary. He issues commands to nature—a wistful relapse into Orphic pretension. Eight imperatives occur within twenty lines, and there is a surprisingly long chain of command within the delicate fancy: the speaker commands the streams, and the streams are to command the vales, and the vales are to command the flowers ('Bid amaranthus all his beauty shed'). The purpose of all this accumulation of flowers—'to strew the laureate hearse'—is withheld for eighteen lines while the mourner solaces himself by enriching and prolonging the catalogue (it is significant that Milton inserted nine lines into this passage in manuscript). The flowers are to be cast 'hither', a meaningless direction in a poem which exists so exclusively in the mind's eye. Descriptions that botanists might have recognized (the 'rathe' primrose,[44] the tufted crow-toe) merge via the 'pale jessamine' and 'glowing violet' into flowers which are half humanized: cowslips hang the pensive head like Herrick's greensick girls, daffodils weep, the woodbine is 'well attired', and plants in 'sad embroidery' are summoned. The pansy—'that's for thoughts'—*freaked* with jet epitomizes the caprice within the wistful mourning, a desire to flatter oneself with the power of fancy. Even the immortal amaranth is to shed all beauty.[45] It is

[43] Bion, *Lament for Adonis*, 75–6. See also Radbertus, Sannazaro and Marot (Harrison, pp. 59, 107, 143–4). Marot is representative: '*Chascune soit d'en porter attentive,/Puis sur la tumbe en jectez bien espais.*'

[44] 'Rathe' was a technical term (see *Variorum*).

[45] The amaranth does not have the heavenly associations it has in *Paradise Lost* in Sannazaro's *Mamillia*, 38 (Harrison, p. 100). But Sannazaro also includes *vivaces amaranthos* in the *aeternos flores* of *Phyllis*, 95 (Harrison, p. 110).

interesting that in re-working this passage Milton omitted the Ovidian cameos that were his first additions ('and that sad floure that strove/to write his owne woes on the vermeil graine'); he wanted a more subtle instance of the fancy enamelling nature.

But the fancy cannot cheat so well. Orphic powers become 'frail thoughts' and 'a little ease' as the mourner acknowledges there is not even a body to deck. His especial agony is that he cannot perform the ritual of a farewell; the body is lost 'under the whelming tide', against which 'moist vows' seem frail indeed. The context is immeasurably stronger here, but it brings to mind the poignancy of Herrick's couplet 'Upon her weeping': 'She by the river sat, and sitting there,/She wept, and made it deeper by a tear,' where the sign of grief seems all the more precious for being so tiny.

However, at least the mourner rejects 'false surmise' and now 'knows the place for the first time'. Moreover, the tremendous lines on the sea which follow and which in prosaic terms lead the mourner to his nadir, are on reflection shot through with hope. For example, the passage contains a unique cluster of verbs beginning the line and hence emphasized. John Reesing has commented that two of these, 'visit'st' and 'sleep'st', 'interject into this picture of mindless, mechanical force a softening note of humanity' (p. 23). This is sensitive, but there is more to say. 'Visit'st' implies that the stay of Lycidas will be temporary and 'sleep'st' that he will awake, and to these can be added the hint of purgation in 'wash'; together they suggest redemption and resurrection rather than humanity, and they anticipate that Lycidas will rise from his 'ocean bed', 'lave' his hair, be 'entertained' by the saints above, and cleansed of grief 'for ever'. Even the term 'bones'—on one level an horrific anticipation of Phlebas the Phoenician—implies, in its mechanical nature, the separation of the true Lycidas from his 'remains'. The crescendo at the lines on the archangel carries some hope within it, since heavenly concern for human affairs—that sense of providence which the mourner has found it so difficult to feel—is implied. The 'guarded mount' may bring Eden to mind, since that *locus amoenissimus* had often been so represented.[46] Although the biblical Eden is most clearly 'guarded' to exclude man after the fall (Gen. 3:24), the location of Michael may hint that England is still an Eden of sorts (especially by comparison with Spain). The 'luckless apple' has been tasted and the sheep are tainted, but heaven is still merciful. Now the imperatives, 'look' and 'waft', are yearning and pleading rather than imperious, and the reference to the dolphins brings to mind the creatures' traditional role as 'a mystic escort of the dead to the Islands of the Blest'.[47]

There is, moreover, a third reason why such apparently despairing lines lead into such exultation: their self-conscious artifice. F.R. Leavis compared the passage unfavourably with Donne's on the 'huge hill' of Truth: 'Though the words are doing so much less work than in Donne, they seem to value themselves more highly . . . What predominates in the handling of them is not the tension of something precise to be defined and fixed, but a concern for mellifluousness' (pp. 52–3). Analysis so far has already shown the inadequacy of this, but Leavis is responding, however harshly, to something that is there. A brief comparison of one or two of the more rebellious poems of Herbert with the more passionate religious sonnets of Donne may help. However carefully crafted they in fact were, poems such as 'Batter my heart . . .' and 'Death, be not proud . . .' seem spontaneous overflows. They are set vividly in the present, and they seem explorations, with the speaker not fully in command. Their sonnet form is intricate, but is a familiar and traditional one. Appreciation of their craftmanship is a secondary response. Herbert, on the other hand, recollects his emotion in tranquillity. Even the disaffection of 'The Collar' and 'Denial' is set in the past, and the harmonious resolutions are sweetly predictable. Moreover,

[46] Rajan, *op. cit.*, p. 54. Berkeley, *op. cit.*, p. 98.
[47] Eugenie Strong, cited in *Variorum*, p. 724. Familiar stories such as that of Arion lend general support, of course, but are hardly close enough to constitute an allusion.

Herbert's poems draw attention to themselves as conscious and ingenious artefacts through a striking idiosyncrasy of form. He does not slight his rebellious impulses and he presents them forcefully; yet he has already worked his way through them, and his achieved serenity is expressed in his capacity to turn them into shapely artefacts.

Milton is here closer to Herbert than to Donne. The sea passage is as much 'surmise' as the preceding floral lines. The one fact is the drowning, and the rest comes from the imagination ('where thou perhaps . . .'). The power of the mind is strangely symbolized in the line: 'Sleep'st by the fable of Bellerus old'. Where one expects a place, one is given a fable, and a fable that Milton has himself created, since he 'seems to have invented *Bellerus* from Bellerium, the Roman name for Land's End'.[48] Likewise, the apparition glimpsed by ancient hermits becomes almost palpably present, on continuous guard. But this is not 'false' surmise, because through these lines the mourner is creating for himself and us the reality of the death and so feeling its full impact. The fancy cheats, the imagination creates—a Romantic distinction, perhaps, but one which would not have surprised Sidney, who knew the power of man's 'erected wit'.

Moreover, as in 'The Collar', the exhilaration of artifice prepares us for an abrupt volte-face. The mourner and the poet cannot be separated in this poem, and the poet directs us to his command of his material, as in the 'fable of Bellerus' or the masterly crescendo from two lines ('whilst thee . . .') to three ('Whether beyond . . .') to four ('Or whether thou . . .'), before the concluding apostrophes. Even the powerful use of the 'hurled/world' rhyme testifies to the author's command, because no rhyme in seventeenth-century verse is more tediously predictable in lesser writers.[49] Verbal idiosyncrasies—such as the *shores* which somehow wash the body far

[48] *Variorum*, p. 720.
[49] Herrick, for example, uses the word 'hurled' eight times, always as a rhyme word and always to rhyme with 'world'. Some of the phrasing is painfully strained.

away, or the visit to the 'bottom of the *monstrous* world'—help to charge the passage with dread: land and sea seem alike abominable, and in collusion against man. But these idiosyncrasies confront us also with the poet's power. While the mourner laments, the poet exults, and rather than being 'strangled by art' the poem is liberated by it.

The point is emphasized if one compares 'Lycidas' with that other great pastoral lament, Sidney's 'Ye goatherd gods . . .' Here the 'wailing and immovable monotony' of their double sestina serves to reinforce rather than distance the claustrophobic grief of Strephon and Klaius, since the relentless repetitions of the form insist on the confines of their world.[50] From the psychoanalytic viewpoint of Barbara Currier Bell, 'Lycidas' is to be valued because of the completeness with which it recapitulates a process of grieving—from denial to anger to depression to resolution—which therapists see as uniform and even stereotyped.[51] Her reading shrinks the poem (the principled anger of Peter, for example, becomes a token of irrational hostility), but its very inadequacy demonstrates a contribution of art such as Milton's to our psychic health. As Lamb realized, such a poet 'dreams being awake. He is not possessed by his subject but he has dominion over it.'[52]

For Louis Martz, lines 8–9, 'For Lycidas is dead . . .' rock 'as if in some directionless agony', and such repetition of word or phrase is 'a sign of the poem's anguish' (p. 65). In apprehending the power of the lines, he overlooks their formality and elegance. For Isabel MacCaffrey, the opening of the poem is brutally direct, and indeed the first line breaks with iambic expectations as emphatically as does the first line of *Paradise Lost*. Yet the line also falls symmetrically into three groups of three stresses, each with two heavier and one lighter stress:

[50] William Empson, *Seven Types of Ambiguity* (1930; rpt. Harmondsworth: Penguin, 1961), p. 36 *et seq*.

[51] 'Lycidas and the Stages of Grief', *Literature and Psychology*, 25 (1975), 166–74.

[52] Cited (p. 45) in Lionel Trilling's very pertinent essay, 'Freud and Literature', *The Liberal Imagination: Essays on Literature and Society* (London: Mercury, 1961), pp. 34–57.

'Yet once more/O ye laur'ls/and once more' (even 'and' must
take some stress, because of its metrical position and because
the previous syllable, in fact only a syllabic consonant, is
almost elided away). In such passages Milton's art contains
and masters the emotion even as it releases it. The poignancy
of these lines is equally representative:

> Thee shepherd, thee the woods, and desert caves,
> With wild thyme and the gadding vine o'ergrown,
> And all their echoes mourn.

The dislocation of word-order emphasizes 'thee' and 'mourn'
fittingly, and also expresses the dislocation of nature by the
death. Yet the lines are also a deliberate re-creation of classical
art, echoing the repeated *te . . . te . . .* of passages in Lucretius,
Ovid and Virgil,[53] while the supreme elegance of the re-
grouped sentence counters the sprawl of neglected nature.
Thus 'leisure for fiction' transmutes anguish into form.

This transmutation culminates beautifully in the strict *ottava
rima* ending. The lines might almost conclude dozens of other
eclogues, and in isolation they would not be striking, but they
are profoundly satisfying as one of the most 'composed' passages in the elegy.

The sudden distancing of the song into the past and into the
words of the 'uncouth swain' symbolizes the gaining of
detachment and serenity. It is, of course, the more sudden
because no pastoral lament had switched so unpredictably
from first- to third-person. Singing 'to the oaks and rills'
brings out both the swain's solitude—Lycidas is dead and
pastoral fellowship has still to be regained—and his common
humanity: he is not Orpheus. He is back in the everyday
world, but is resolved and accepting. The sun no longer flames
in the forehead of the sky; the morning is now grey, but calm
and still—the 'felon winds' are not on the loose. His 'tender'
music has the frailty of man, but is also sensitive and respon-

---

[53] Leishman, *op. cit.*, pp. 325–6, cites *De Rerum Natura*, I, 6, *Metamorphoses*,
XI, 43–5, and *Georgics*, IV, 465–6, to which *Ecl.* I, 38–9 can be added.

sive, and, being 'various', it clearly does not lack range. His contemplation of life is no longer reluctant, but is 'eager', and his fingers are delicate rather than 'forced' and 'rude'. His lay is 'Doric', not only in allusion to the supposed rusticity of pastoral but to the mode of ancient music:

> the Dorian mood
> Of flutes and soft recorders; such as raised
> To height of noblest temper heroes old
> Arming to battle, and in stead of rage
> Deliberate valour breathed, firm and unmoved
> With dread of death to flight or foul retreat;
> Nor wanting power to mitigate and swage,
> With solemn touches, troubled thoughts, and chase
> Anguish and doubt and fear and sorrow and pain
> From mortal or immortal minds.
> (*Paradise Lost*, I, 550–9)[54]

Again there is a daily cycle which almost seems to suspend time ('And now . . . And now . . .'). The sun stretching out all the hills is a characteristic estrangement and intensification of pastoral norms, where sunset heralds the end of the poem:

> *maioresque cadunt altis de montibus umbrae (Ecl.* I, 83)

> *et sol crescentes decedens duplicat umbras (Ecl.* II, 67)[55]

In the previous paragraph the sun became associated with the raised Lycidas, and there is almost a hint of the faith that can move mountains in the stretching out of *hills* rather than of shadows. But in the next line the passive replaces the active, and the sun is dropped, as Lycidas was, into the sea. The 'western bay' is almost consoling after 'each beakéd promontory' and 'the bottom of the monstrous world', but neverthe-

---

[54] See Plato, *Republic,* III, 398–9. Clay Hunt, *Lycidas and the Italian Critics* (New Haven & London: Yale University Press, 1979), pp. 123, 149–50 & 165, has some comments on Dorian music.

[55] 'and longer shadows fall from the mountain-heights'; 'and the retiring sun doubles the lengthening shadows'.

less Lycidas *is* dead, and this has to be lived with. The sense of loss and of gain alike lives in the memory of the now resolved soul, as the repeated 'now' implies, with the abrupt shift it brings into the historical present. As the sun drops, the swain rises decisively, and his sudden motion brings not only a flash of colour into the subdued ending, but also symbolic hints of hope and truth.[56] The last line is a quiet but typically audacious redirection of pastoral. A sense of belonging makes return home the traditional ending of an eclogue—almost all the months of *The Shepherd's Calendar* end this way, for example. Meliboeus, the displaced farmer of Virgil's first Eclogue, is wretched and embittered. But Milton and his solitary swain face the new experience that must be theirs resiliently and with faith restored, thanks to the power of art.

[56] See *Variorum*. Ben Jonson's figure Omothymia or Unanimity in *The King's Entertainment (Works*, ed. C.H. Herford and P. & E. Simpson, Oxford: Clarendon Press, 1925–52), VII, 89, lines 197 ff., is dressed all in blue, 'shewing one trueth and intireness of minde'. See also *Works* IV, 133 ('*bluenesse* doth expresse truenesse') and VII, 84–5 and 233.